"The story of Corrie ten Boom is timeless, and I'm grateful that Stan Guthrie's new book, *Victorious,* is reawakening a fascination with this remarkable woman's witness. I was in my early 20s when I grew to know and love 'Tante Corrie,' and her tender, yet no-nonsense way of walking with her beloved Jesus helped shape my own life story. Her last words, spoken to me in her thick Dutch accent? 'Joni, one day we shall dance together in heaven!' And I'm still waiting for that dance. Turn the page and get to know this saint-of-the-age, as well as the history and details behind her amazing testimony. Her life may end up shaping your story, too!"
    —**Joni Eareckson Tada,** Joni and Friends International Disability Center

"Corrie ten Boom's faith and courage during World War II are on full display in her classic book, *The Hiding Place,* and in my own writings I've made no secret of my tremendous admiration for her. But Stan Guthrie's book, *Victorious,* demonstrates Corrie's continuing relevance for many current challenges, including refugees, anti-Semitism, and sharing the love of God in a skeptical age. Highly recommended."
    —**Eric Metaxas,** #1 *New York Times* bestselling author of
    Bonhoeffer: Pastor, Martyr, Prophet, Spy,
    7 Women: And the Secret of Their Greatness,
    and host of the nationally syndicated *Eric Metaxas Radio Show*

"I grew up on *The Hiding Place.* Not only did our family read it; we told and retold each other the harrowing stories from the book's pages. In the process, Corrie ten Boom's powerful, real-life account of faith and forgiveness in the face of unspeakable evil shaped my imagination. I am far from alone. The book has impacted millions, and now Guthrie, a skilled journalist and historian, is helping us understand why. With fascinating details about Corrie's life, and insight into post-war evangelicalism, Guthrie paints a vivid picture of the wider world into which the book was born. *Victorious* will intrigue people who have never read *The Hiding Place.* And it will enable those of us who have read it, to encounter it again for the first time."
    —**Drew Dyck,** author of *Your Future Self Will Thank You: Secrets to Self-Control from the Bible and Brain Science*

"Stan Guthrie has brought one of our modern-day evangelical 'saints' to vivid life. He skillfully weaves 'Tante Corrie's' riveting story of extraordinary bravery to the glory of God with our all-too-human story as contemporary followers of Jesus wrestling with profound 'how should we then live?' issues. On the way he brings in a snapshot of postwar America, Billy Graham, Hollywood, the scourge of anti-Semitism, and so much more. Highly recommended."

—Elizabeth Cody Newenhuyse,
author of *God, I Know You're Here Somewhere*

"Stan Guthrie paints a moving portrait of Christian Holocaust survivor and evangelist Corrie ten Boom, and details how her relationships with the likes of Brother Andrew and John and Elizabeth Sherrill led to one of the remarkable books of the 20th century. Guthrie also helps us apply Corrie's life and ministry to the issues the church faces today: from evangelism, to anti-Semitism, to care for the elderly, immigration, and more. This book is a unique and compelling combination of biography, church history, and applied Christian worldview."

—John Stonestreet,
President of the Colson Center for Christian Worldview,
and host of *BreakPoint*

STAN GUTHRIE

VICTORIOUS

Corrie ten Boom and *The Hiding Place*

PARACLETE PRESS

BREWSTER, MASSACHUSETTS

2019 First Printing
Victorious: Corrie ten Boom and The Hiding Place

Copyright © 2019 by Stan Guthrie

ISBN 978-1-64060-175-8

The Paraclete Press name and logo (dove on cross) are trademarks of Paraclete Press, Inc.

Library of Congress Cataloging-in-Publication Data
Names: Guthrie, Stan, author.
Title: Victorious: Corrie ten Boom and the Hiding place / Stan Guthrie.
Description: Brewster, Massachusetts: Paraclete Press, 2019. | "Guthrie
  explores the spiritual, historical, and cultural context behind Corrie ten
  Boom's memoir--the "triumphant true story" of her experiences during World
  War II, including her imprisonment by the Nazis, that has inspired more
  than 3 million readers"--Provided by publisher. | Includes bibliographical
  references and index.
Identifiers: LCCN 2019010147 | ISBN 9781640601758 (hardcover, dj)
Subjects: LCSH: Ten Boom, Corrie. Hiding place. | Ten Boom,
  Corrie--Appreciation.
Classification: LCC D811.5 .T42734 2019 | DDC 943.53/492092--dc23
LC record available at https://lccn.loc.gov/2019010147

10 9 8 7 6 5 4 3 2 1

Published by Paraclete Press
Brewster, Massachusetts
www.paracletepress.com

Printed in the United States of America

For Benedict and Everild
*May you find
in Jesus the Victor
your own hiding place.*

Contents

ONE

The Context

No book, and certainly not *The Hiding Place*, emerges ex nihilo, like Venus from the sea. Though the gospel it shares and the Savior it exalts are timeless, Corrie ten Boom's 1971 classic could not have sold millions of copies and helped shape the faith of a generation by itself. A number of specific people, events, and issues came together providentially to provide a bracing wind for this unforgettable volume's literary sails. Nearly half a century on, *The Hiding Place* still thrills and challenges us with its portrait of an imperfect servant of Jesus the Victor determined to defy evil, defend the weak, and endure hardship.

CHAPTER 1

A DIZZYING ERA

The Hiding Place tells the story of several members of a close-knit, godly Christian family in Nazi-occupied Holland who choose to hide Jews, are betrayed by neighbors, and ultimately are sent to concentration camps, where several members of the family perish, and those who live are brought closer to Christ. Corrie, the first-person voice of this spiritual memoir, wrestles with issues such as renunciation of one's plans for God's, the ethics of lying to an evil regime to protect the innocent, how to forgive one's persecutors, how to discern the light of hope when all around is in shadows, and how to go on with life after calamity. The book ends within months of the war's close, with Corrie, already well into middle age, starting a ministry of reconciliation and healing first envisioned by her older, wiser (and now deceased) sister, Betsie.

The book's impact has been immense, its message timeless. Evangelical author Philip Yancey called *The Hiding Place* "a groundbreaking book that shines a clear light on one of the darkest moments of history." Jack W. Hayford, president of the International Foursquare Church, said it "is even more relevant to the present hour than at the time of its writing." Joyce Meyer, the well-known Bible teacher, said that *The Hiding Place* "is a classic that begs revisiting."[1] That is what we will do, God willing, in this volume.

The story told in *The Hiding Place* ends just before the start of a dizzying quarter-century of ministry for Corrie in scores of countries, and on the cusp of a still-challenging time for the world in which she worked. First were the early, painful years of rebuilding in Europe, along with the shock of discovery of the scale of Nazi atrocities. In the United States, the postwar boom commenced from a mobilized industrial base and pent-up consumer demand from people who had scrimped in the national effort to turn back tyranny. Corrie soon discovered that evangelicals in America largely were more open to her message of reconciliation and spiritual encouragement than were Christians in many parts of the Continent, where her story began.

America quickly assumed a hard-won central role on the global stage. Just as quickly, however, the nation was faced with the limits of its power. It was a time of increasing material prosperity and living standards, as well as new educational opportunities through the G.I. Bill. But it was also a time in which many Americans made an inward turn. A second world war had shocked them. Questions of theodicy and doubt—*How could a loving God allow such things to happen?*—arose in the hearts of the faithful. People wanted to get back to their dogged pursuit of happiness in what theological optimists still hoped was an "American Century," forgetting about the horrors perpetrated in foreign lands.

However, the Cold War brought a new enemy, international communism, in the form of the Union of Soviet Socialist Republics and, soon thereafter, Red China. The Korean War followed quickly, ending in stalemate, and the world watched as the British Empire collapsed, ushering in unexpected forms of nationalism and popular unrest around the world. France's eventual withdrawal from French Indochina would lead to another bloody impasse and, eventually, to defeat for an America that had promised to "pay any price, bear any burden, meet any hardship, support any friend, oppose any foe to assure the survival and the success of liberty."[2] Apparently, the price was simply too high for an America with myriad challenges at home. Corrie had known well the vagaries of international affairs and how quickly they can turn one's comfortable home life upside down. It was a message for which many Americans were becoming increasingly ripe, though they did not yet know this.

The sixties in America began in optimism and ended, for many, in disillusionment. John F. Kennedy asked the citizens of an idealistic, confident nation to consider not what their country could do for them, but what they could do for their country. That kind of other-centered optimism was soon to dissipate. At first the country experienced another round of roaring economic growth, which in large part paid for the audacious Apollo program to put a man on the moon (while staving off a feared Soviet domination of outer space). Government ambitions were stratospheric in other ways, as well. The Johnson administration offered up the Great Society in an attempt to level the playing field for oppressed minorities and put an end to poverty.

The civil rights movement, too, sought to persuade a nation to live up to the ideals in its founding documents and dismantle Jim Crow, granting people of color the same civil rights as white people. It was powered by the soaring rhetoric of the Rev. Martin Luther King Jr., who had a dream that all God's children, of whatever race, would come together as brothers and sisters. King and others who stood up for racial equality, echoing Moses, to "let my people go," often were met with arrest, jail, and water cannons, but eventually they prevailed. While Corrie would become famous primarily for her courage in hiding Jews and forgiving her enemies, her personal biography of ministering to young people, those with disabilities, and people of many nationalities would provide a nonthreatening model for Americans grappling with reconciliation and cultural diversity issues.

The civil rights record for evangelicals, Christians who "take the Bible seriously and believe in Jesus Christ as Savior and Lord,"[3] is tragically mixed on this score. Historian David Bebbington has offered a widely accepted four-part definition of evangelical characteristics.[4] They are conversionism (the belief that people must be transformed through belief in Christ and a lifetime of following him); activism (the gospel must be demonstrated through missionary work and social reform); biblicism (a high regard for the Bible and a desire to obey it as the final authority in life); and crucicentrism (a stress on the Cross of Christ as the basis of salvation). While Corrie, coming out of the Dutch Reformed Church, could not be classified as a card-carrying evangelical, these four points resonated with her and gave her an open door to speak into the hearts of the huge American evangelical audience. They were hearts that needed encouragement and challenge, and Corrie would provide both.

While each of these four points, as well as the long history of Christian social reform[5] and the example of Jesus himself, support a commitment to racial equality, too often evangelicals in this era looked the other way, like the priest and the Levite in the parable of the good Samaritan.[6] "Evangelicals resisted black equality in many ways," Carolyn Renée Dupont, associate professor of history at Eastern Kentucky University, told Justin Taylor of the Gospel Coalition. "Some ministers preached an overt biblical sanction for segregation. Most preachers took a more oblique approach, remaining silent about black equality while condemning faith-based civil rights activism as 'a prostitution of the church

Corrie ten Boom discovered that evangelicals in America were more open to her message than were their counterparts in many parts of the Continent.

for political purposes.' Most southern Christians did not regard segregation as a sin, and they resented those who criticized their 'way of life.'"[7]

A notable exception was Billy Graham, the international evangelist from North Carolina, who would become a strong friend and promoter of Corrie. Lon Allison, former executive director of the Billy Graham Center at Wheaton College, says in *Billy Graham: An Ordinary Man and His Extraordinary God* that early in Graham's ministry, in 1952 in Jackson, Mississippi, or in 1953 in Chattanooga, Tennessee, the evangelist personally pulled down the ropes separating blacks and whites at his crusades.[8] From that point on, all would hear the gospel together, as equals before God and man.

Some have chided Graham for not doing more during the struggle for civil rights. Scholar Steven P. Miller calls him a "racial moderate" when compared with Martin Luther King Jr., and indeed Graham sought a heart change through the gospel as the ultimate answer to racism, not legislation.[9] Graham, however, explained that his emphasis on gospel preaching was supported by King, who shared the platform at Graham's New York crusade in 1957.

"Early on," Graham said, "Dr. King and I spoke about his method of using nonviolent demonstrations to bring an end to racial segregation. He urged me to keep on doing what I was doing— preaching the Gospel to integrated audiences and supporting his goals by example, and not to join him in the streets. 'You stay in the stadiums, Billy,' he said, because you will have far more impact on the white establishment there than you would if you marched in the streets. . . . But if a leader gets too far ahead of his people, they will lose sight of him and not follow him any longer.' I followed his advice."[10] Like Corrie, Graham emphasized the need for a change of heart through the Good News to overcome the sin of racism rather than a social or political program.

Civil rights was far from the only issue roiling the American landscape, and the comfortable cultural perch on which many evangelical believers sat. Among them were widespread campus radicalism, race riots, Vietnam, the drug and hippie cultures, several shocking political assassinations, and growing demands from feminists for equal rights. The America that had seemed so welcoming in previous decades suddenly seemed alien to many people. Corrie, whose native country had been overwhelmed by the Nazi invasion, could relate.

In the comparative historical blip between victory in the Second World War and the unraveling in Vietnam, old verities were being challenged, sometimes violently, as new, sometimes alien, values came to the fore. During the "Me Decade" of the seventies, Watergate, inflation, the war, "no-fault" divorce, and other troubles sapped people's willingness to trust, and to reach out. Many were simply hoping for a breather. Evangelicals were concerned with the spiritual and social upheaval they were seeing in America.

They were far from alone. The decade brought many challenges. Crime rates were rising. The brutal, unhinged Manson family shocked the nation. The year 1971 was filled with challenges and controversies—the continuing Cold War, the Pentagon Papers, racial unrest and rioting, the Attica prison riot, the Weather Underground, and the controversial Equal Rights Amendment approved by the US House.

The early seventies would be full of disorienting and unwelcome challenges for evangelicals and the heretofore self-confident country in which they lived. Inflation, fueled by federal monetary policies and other factors, more than doubled to 8.8 percent. In a few years, it would hit 12 percent. By 1980, the inflation rate was 14 percent.[11] American Christians unknowingly were being prepared to receive Corrie's message of faithfulness amid times of national distress.

The international scene also was unsettled. The Arab oil embargo, sparked in October 1973 by the Nixon administration's support of Israel in the Yom Kippur War, drove the price of a barrel of oil from $2.90 to $11.65,[12] raising the price at the pump for a gallon of gasoline from 38.5 cents to 55.1 cents. Facing oil shortages, many states asked citizens not to put up Christmas lights. Oregon banned them.[13] Other shocks were not long in coming: Watergate, the painful loss of South Vietnam to the communists, the decline of traditional American manufacturing power and the automakers, and American foreign policy and prestige foundering under the "born again" president, Jimmy Carter.

The Supreme Court's *Roe v. Wade* decision legalizing abortion across all fifty states was still two years away. President Richard Nixon, seeking to justify his policies, had claimed the support of a "silent majority," and evangelicals were a big part of his coalition, and that of George Wallace in Alabama. While the Religious Right and Moral Majority were not yet formed, evangelicals were beginning to organize politically at the local level. Corrie's story, however, demonstrated the limits of political solutions in the face of evil. Though she was bold enough to confront it or resist it, Corrie's goal was always to advance the kingdom of Jesus the Victor, not any earthly kingdom. It was an approach that would resonate with American Christians struggling with big challenges.

Television was also changing, transitioning rapidly from a medium whose primary aim was entertainment of the masses to sell advertising to one in which social change was preached in subtle, and not so subtle, ways. While there was still plenty of fluff to go around (*Happy Days, Welcome Back, Kotter*, and *Charlie's Angels*, for example), increasing numbers of programs were developing a harder social edge, broaching topics that had once been confined to the campus, the dinner table, or the bedroom.

Concerning depictions of the Second World War in film and television, 1961's engrossing *Judgment at Nuremberg* depicted the trial of four German judges for cooperating with the Nazis and committing crimes against humanity. The film won numerous awards and is notable for its groundbreaking use of grisly Allied film of slaughtered concentration-camp victims. Among the many other movies depicting the conflict were *Sink the Bismarck!* (1960), *The Guns of Navarone* (1961), and *Battle of the Bulge* (1965).

In America, acknowledgment of the Holocaust, which had left six million Jews dead, was not high on the agenda. In 1945, General Dwight D. Eisenhower, Supreme Allied Commander, had visited a concentration camp in the ancient German city of Gotha. Eisenhower wanted to collect evidence of the German slaughter of Jews while it was still fresh, to preclude people from denying the enormity of what the Germans had perpetrated. "I visited every nook and cranny of the camp," Eisenhower said, "because I felt it my duty to be in a position from then on to testify at first hand about these things in case there ever grew up at home the belief or assumption that 'the stories of Nazi brutality were just propaganda.'"[14]

The tendency to pass over the horror of the Holocaust and get on with life was strong in 1960s America. Even worse, anti-Semitism was little discussed but very much alive. According to the Anti-Defamation League of B'nai B'rith, in 1964, a disturbing 29 percent of American adults held anti-Semitic views.[15]

Anne Frank: The Diary of a Young Girl was first published in 1952. The book was a sensation in personalizing the persecution and murder of Jews by the Nazis. Through the pen of young Anne in her diary, it describes how a Jewish family hid in some secret rooms in an Amsterdam office building. The book spotlights the developing and sometimes difficult relationships of ordinary people trying to live ordinary lives in desperate circumstances. Their betrayal and capture are not presented, except briefly in an epilogue. The horrifying *Night* (English edition, 1960), by Holocaust survivor Elie Wiesel, also roused some in America from their complacency.

But not all. The farcical television comedy *Hogan's Heroes* (1965–1971) was ending its long run on CBS. The series portrayed an international group of Allied prisoners running special operations out of a German POW camp, Stalag 13. Four of the major German characters were actually portrayed by Jewish actors, and three of them, and one other supporting actor, were Jews who had escaped from the Nazis during World War II. While the Nazis on *Hogan's Heroes* were usually presented as inept or evil (or both), there was no grappling with the extent of horror perpetrated by the Third Reich, and the word "Jew" was never mentioned. Corrie's story would challenge such complacency by showing Christian boldness in the face of explicit Nazi evil.

In terms of religious affiliation, the postwar era was seeing a gradual but noticeable decline in the number of Americans claiming to be Protestant or other non-Catholic adherents of Christianity.[16] From a high above 70 percent in the mid- to late 1950s, their share had slipped to 61 percent by 1973, owing to a more welcoming attitude toward Roman Catholics in the nation's mainstream and to a change in federal immigration policy that brought in fewer immigrants from Europe and more from Asia and Latin America.[17]

In this time of social upheaval, cultural diversity, and declining influence, Protestant evangelicals were ripe for reassurance about old truths. They were also looking for new heroes, and the explosion onto the national scene of one James Earl Carter was still years away.[18] But two such heroes, from the Netherlands of all places, were already working among them.

CHAPTER 2

—

RELIGION, JEWS, AND THE "EVIL EMPIRE"

The country's "long twilight struggle"[1] against communism was much more than a political and military challenge for the nation's leaders. It was also ideological and religious, for the masses. According to the Dwight D. Eisenhower Library, "During the Cold War years religion was seen by many as playing an important role in the struggle against Communism."[2] The atheism that was integral to Marxism was a direct challenge to the monotheism of Judaism and Christianity, with many of their followers facing prison and exile during the Cold War for their beliefs. This reality will play a significant role in understanding Corrie ten Boom and the success of her book, which highlighted a faithful Christian's response to another totalitarian system seeking to usurp the place of God in people's lives—and which also targeted the Jewish people.

Billy Graham often spoke about the challenge of communism in his crusades. In a 1951 message, "Christianism vs. Communism," the evangelist cited Eisenhower's military buildup but counseled listeners to put their trust in Christ above everything else. "Throughout the entire world at this moment, Christianity and communism are battling for the minds of men," Graham said. "The outcome will determine what kind of world the next generation will live in."[3]

Many other religious leaders called on Americans in the postwar years to embrace Christian faith as a bulwark against the atheism espoused by what would soon be called an "evil empire."[4] Eisenhower wasn't too particular about *which* faith, saying, "Our form of government makes no sense unless it is founded in a deeply felt religious belief, and I don't care what it is."[5]

Guideposts magazine, founded in 1945 by Norman Vincent Peale, author of the bestseller *The Power of Positive Thinking*, and his wife, Ruth Stafford Peale, was a popular expression of a growing nonsectarian religious faith in America. The magazine welcomed contributions from Protestants, Catholics, and Jews on how God makes a difference in life. Two talented and thorough Christian writers, the married couple John and Elizabeth Sherrill, honed their craft at and devoted most of their careers to *Guideposts*.

The Sherrills also wrote books—and not just any books, but bestsellers. In 1962 they told the story of David Wilkerson in *The Cross and the Switchblade*. In their travels they also came across a Dutch Christian named Andrew van der Bijl, who had played a small part in the Dutch underground. After World War II, van der Bijl was wounded in the war for independence in the Dutch East Indies (later, Indonesia). During his rehabilitation, van der Bijl converted to Christianity and became concerned for suffering Christians behind the Iron Curtain.

Thus began a ministry in which van der Bijl, soon to be known simply as Brother Andrew, smuggled Bibles into countries such as Poland, Russia, and China to support fellow believers in places where owning a Bible was forbidden. It was 1955, in the thick of the Cold War, when Andrew began his ministry in Poland.

Brother Andrew's story of Christian heroism dovetailed perfectly with the anti-communist, pro-Christian mood in the United States. The Sherrills, drawn to human-interest stories with a faith angle, met Andrew during his travels for Open Doors, the ministry he founded to help persecuted Christians. The Sherrills were expert reporters and wordsmiths who knew how to draw out Andrew's story in thrilling detail.

The result, in 1967, was *God's Smuggler*.[6] Open Doors recounts an event from early in Andrew's smuggling ministry, also described in the book:

On this occasion, Brother Andrew approached the Romanian border in his car—which was packed with illegal Bibles.

He could only hope the border guards were moving swiftly and not paying much attention, which might allow him to pass through undetected.

But just as he was hoping this, Brother Andrew saw the guards stop the car at the front of the line. He watched, in anticipation, as the vehicle's owners were forced to take out all of the car's contents and spread them on the ground for inspection.

Each car that followed received the same treatment, with the fourth car's inspection lasting the longest. The guard took a full hour to sift through it, including removing hubcaps, taking the engine apart, and even removing the seats.

"Dear Lord," Brother Andrew remembers praying, "What am I going to do?"

As he prayed, a bold idea came to Brother Andrew. "I know that no amount of cleverness on my part can get me through this border search. Dare I ask for a miracle? Let me take some of the Bibles out and leave them in the open where they will be seen."

Putting the Bibles out in the open would truly be depending on God, rather than his own intelligence, he thought. So when the guards ushered Andrew forward, he did just this. "I handed him my papers and started to get out. But his knee was against the door, holding it closed."

And then, the almost unbelievable happened.

The guard looked at Brother Andrew's passport and abruptly waved him on. "Surely thirty seconds had not passed," he remembers.

Brother Andrew started the engine and began pulling away, all the while wondering if he was supposed to pull over so the car could be taken apart and examined. "I coasted forward, my foot poised above the brake. Nothing happened. I looked out the rear mirror. The guard was waving the next car to a stop, indicating to the driver that he had to get out."

God had cleared the way for Brother Andrew to smuggle the Bible to Christians who had no access to God's Word.[7]

James Bond and *The Man from U*N*C*L*E* had nothing on Brother Andrew, and readers have been hooked ever since.[8] Open Doors International estimates that more than ten million copies have been sold, in thirty-five languages.[9]

Another subject capturing the attention of Christians was the Jewish people. Hal Lindsey's 1970 best seller, *The Late Great Planet Earth*, with a decidedly dispensational, premillennial eschatology, was a big reason why. Lindsey, looking at current events, the undeniable threat of the Soviet Union, and the postwar establishment of the state of Israel in the Holy Land, postulated that the "end times" would soon be upon us, complete with the coming of the antichrist and a pre-tribulation rapture of the faithful.

As a result, the Jewish state was much on the minds of America's evangelicals. Larry Eskridge, an independent historian and former director of the Institute for the Study of American Evangelicals at Wheaton College, notes that at the time "the evangelical community was overwhelmingly in the grips of End Times fervor—even as they went about their business in so many other practical ways. Hard on the heels of the seemingly impossible Israeli triumph in the Six-Day War in 1967 and the capture of Jerusalem, the evangelical community was keen about anything that touched upon Jews, Israel, and the Middle East."[10]

Eskridge points to numerous examples of this fervor. "Prophecy books [were] flying off the shelf," he says,[11] citing Lindsey and dispensational icon John Walvoord, as well as the founding of Jews for Jesus by Moishe Rosen, the ministry of Zola Leavitt—another Jewish convert to evangelical faith—and even the Jesus People music scene.

The Jesus People Movement, according to Eskridge, author of *God's Forever Family: The Jesus People Movement in America*,[12] combined the hippie counterculture and evangelical Christianity. It first appeared in San Francisco's Haight-Ashbury district in 1967 before spreading to Southern California, Seattle, Atlanta, and Milwaukee. By 1971, the Jesus People had garnered national media attention and a huge following among evangelical church young people.[13] Meanwhile, Jews for Jesus, founded in San Francisco in 1969, sought to reinvigorate reaching Jewish people with the message of their Messiah, Jesus.[14]

"Bottom line," Eskridge says, "if it had to do with things Jewish, 1970s evangelicals were interested."[15]

After a quarter-century of busy but fairly low-key travels in the United States, Europe, and elsewhere, Corrie ten Boom had sown the seeds of a hopeful Christian message of love for the Jewish people in the midst of horrific human evil. Her coming entrance onto the wider evangelical stage would be providentially timed for maximum impact for her yet-to-be-written book. "I think [*The Hiding Place*] dovetails nicely with this [interest in the Jews]," Eskridge says, "because of its focus on a pietist,[16] evangelical-ish Christian who [stepped] up to help Jews in their time of need—a broad theme that evangelicals [saw] as a political, as well as a personal, question."[17]

It is to this "pietist, evangelical-ish" Christian woman that we now turn.

TWO

The Creation

The Hiding Place begins in 1937, as the ten Booms prepare to celebrate the one-hundredth anniversary of the family's watchmaking and repair business in Haarlem. But the story started much earlier. How this story was told and retold over the decades says much about the author, about us, and about the providence of God.

CHAPTER 3

—

A BOOK
IS LIVED

Isaac da Costa was a prolific Jewish poet and scholar from Amsterdam with an interest in Jesus. "I began to read the New Testament," he said. "I began to feel an abhorrence of sin for which the Savior Himself, manifested in the flesh, had suffered the death of the cross. I realized the fulfilment of the prophecies of Isaiah 11, 53, 61, and in Psalms 22 and 110. I adored, I believed and slowly this faith worked on my conscience and my behavior changed. Religion was no longer merely a sublime speculation, or a great national interest. I found that I must become the property of Jesus Christ, that I must live to Him, and by Him."

Da Costa, his wife, Hannah Belmonte, and a friend were baptized in 1822 in Leiden.[1] Soon Da Costa began to make a name for himself in another way—by speaking out against the tide of theological skepticism and moral laxity sweeping across the continent. One of his books was titled *Objections Against the Spirit of This Age*. Da Costa's call was met with widespread derision, but a small group of Dutch Christians agreed with him. One of them was named Willem ten Boom, Corrie's grandfather.[2]

Their numbers began to grow, and soon the Netherlands began experiencing a massive revival that returned the Bible to its rightful place as the authoritative Word of God. But Da Costa wasn't finished. He hoped to spark a renewed Christian outreach across Europe to the Jewish people.

"We all agree that a strong bond ties us to Israel," Da Costa said at the 1851 World Conference of the Evangelical Alliance in London. "As to the past, Christianity is a fruit, an offshoot from the old people of God. As to the present, is not Israel's existence among the nations, despite centuries of hostility and persecution, one of the strongest proofs against the world's unbelief? And as to the future, how clearly the fulfillment of God's promises is related to the future of the world and the coming Kingdom of Christ! For these reasons I dare come to you with an earnest plea. It is a custom in Israel at certain great feasts to keep an open seat for the prophet Elijah. I request that you keep an open seat for Israel in our midst today."[3]

During the nineteenth century, more and more Jewish people saw the need to establish a permanent homeland in the Holy Land. In 1844 Willem ten Boom (1816–1891) founded a group to "pray for the peace of Jerusalem." He became one of the founders of the Society for Israel,[4] and he taught his family to love the Jewish people as well. His son, Casper (1859–1944), later said, "Love for the Jews was spoon-fed to me from my very youngest years."[5]

In 1837, Willem had rented space for the ten Boom Horlogerie (watch shop) at Barteljorisstraat 19, called the Beje ("bay-yay"), in Haarlem. In 1841, he married Geertruida van Gogh. In 1849, he bought the Beje, with room for the shop and for living quarters, for 1,200 guilders. Geertruida died of tuberculosis in 1856, and, in 1858, Willem married Elisabeth Bel. Their oldest child, Casper, was born the following year.

At age twenty-five, Casper married Cornelia Luitingh, and their children were born in quick succession (Elisabeth, or "Betsie," in 1885; Willem in 1886; Hendrik Jan in 1888 [he died in 1889]; Arnolda Johanna, or "Nollie," in 1890; and Cornelia Arnolda Johanna, "Corrie," on April 15, 1892).[6] The children's grandfather, Willem, died in 1891, but what he taught the family lasted a lifetime.

The years leading up to the family's centennial celebration in 1937 at Barteljorisstraat 19, Haarlem, were full of faith and family. In 1897, Grandmother Elisabeth moved out of what Elizabeth Sherrill calls "the crooked old house in Haarlem,"[7] so that Casper and his young family could move in. The Beje was actually two old houses joined together. Corrie's bedroom was in the second "house," up the stairs and farthest from the front door.

That same year Corrie, at age five, gave her life to Jesus. "Jesus said that He is standing at the door," Corrie's mother told her, "and if you invite Him in, He will come into your heart. Would you like Jesus in?" Corrie replied in childlike faith, "Yes, Mama, I want Jesus in my heart."[8] Jesus Christ was central to the ten Booms' existence. In the family dining room was a tile that read, *Jezus is Overwinnaar*, "Jesus is Victor."[9] The saying would guide Corrie her entire life.[10]

The saying might have reflected the influence of the contemporary Swedish Lutheran theologian Gustaf Aulèn, who was advancing the argument that Martin Luther and the church fathers believed in the *Christus Victor* theory of Christ's Atonement. The theory emphasizes the truth that Christ's death on the cross and resurrection defeated the rule of Satan over believers and brought us freedom. Aulèn, in his book *Christus Victor*, preferred this explanation over the substitutionary atonement and the moral exemplar theories. Aulèn wrote, "The work of Christ is first and foremost a victory over the powers which hold mankind in bondage: sin, death, and the devil."[11]

As well, the saying may have reflected the continuing cultural influence of the Flemish (Dutch-speaking) master Peter Paul Rubens (1577–1640), whose powerful work *Christus als overwinnaar van Satan en de Dood* (Christ triumphant over Satan and Death)[12] is still highlighted by the Netherlands Institute for Art History in The Hague. The ten Booms would have resonated with the conviction of both Aulèn and Rubens that Jesus is victorious over the powers of evil, particularly as that evil would manifest itself in the days ahead.

Corrie completed primary and secondary school before studying at the Domestic Science School. In 1909, the ten Booms started a missions study group in their home. Corrie took classes at a Bible school for two years starting in 1910 and, after failing her final exam, would receive her diploma eight years later.

In 1916, Willem was ordained and called to a church in Made. He soon married Tine van Veen, the daughter of the family doctor. Their son Kik was born in 1920. That same year, Corrie completed a demanding watchmaking apprenticeship in Switzerland. The next year, when her mother died, Corrie began working full-time in the shop. In 1924, she became the country's first licensed female watchmaker.

The family's Christian faith continued to express itself in practical expressions of love. They began to take in missionary children in 1925. There were seven foster children living at the Beje, and they were affectionately known as the Red Cap Club.

Though she had no children of her own, Corrie led Bible classes in the public schools and taught Sunday school at church. Corrie also organized and ran a network of clubs, first for girls and then for both girls and boys, under the sponsorship of the Union des Amies de la Jeune Fille. She was one of the leaders of the movement in Holland. However, she eventually came to believe that the clubs were losing their Christian emphasis, so she formed

De Nederlandse Meisjesclubs (The Dutch Girls Club), which she continued to lead until 1940, when the Germans invaded Holland and outlawed group meetings.[13] Many of her young charges would call her *Tante* Corrie, or Aunt Corrie.

After accepting a pastorate in the picturesque town of Zuylen, Willem began studying anti-Semitism at the nearby university in Utrecht, where he soon discovered his true calling. "I was captivated by the subject of anti-Semitism from the start," he told Tine, "but now that I am really getting into it, it is taking possession of me. I can no longer get away from it. The Jewish question is haunting me. It is so dangerous. Anti-Semitism has repercussions which will affect the whole world."[14]

In 1926, he began working with the Society for Israel. Studying for one year in Leipzig, Germany, he received a doctorate in philosophy in 1928. His thesis topic was racial anti-Semitism.[15] At the time of the centennial celebration, he was in charge of the Dutch Reformed Church's outreach to Jews. "Dear Willem," Corrie wrote later. "If he's converted a single Jew in twenty years, I'd not heard about it."[16] Willem actively served the Jewish people nonetheless, constructing a home for elderly Jews in Hilversum—a home that became a haven for more and more desperate Jews as the situation in Germany deteriorated.[17]

Despite the darkening prospects for Jews across Europe, the centennial celebration at the watch shop was attended not only by Corrie's family but by seemingly the entire neighborhood, Gentile *and* Jew. Among the Jewish people at the party were Mr. and Mrs. Kans, who ran a competing watch shop down the street, and Herr Gutileber, who had just escaped from Germany in the back of a milk truck.[18]

Casper was warmly regarded by all his neighbors, and by Jewish colleagues across the Netherlands. In *The Hiding Place*,

Corrie recounts how, on her first day of school, she had decided to stay home with the women. Rather than argue, Casper simply grasped his reluctant daughter by the hand and marched her, gently but firmly, to her school and into the wide world.

Often Corrie's father would take her on other trips, such as his weekly visits to Amsterdam to get the exact time at the Naval Observatory. On these trips they would reserve plenty of time to visit with watch wholesalers he knew, many of whom were Jewish.

"After the briefest possible discussion of business," Corrie writes, "Father would draw out a small Bible from his traveling case; the wholesaler, whose beard would be even longer and fuller than Father's, would snatch a book or a scroll out of a drawer, clap a prayer cap onto his head; and the two of them would be off, arguing, comparing, interrupting, contradicting—reveling in each other's company."[19]

Casper ten Boom's kindness and moral stature loom large in *The Hiding Place*. His jaunts into Amsterdam with young Corrie provided other spiritual lessons that served her well when the Nazi trial by fire came. Once, when Corrie was ten or eleven, she came across what she thought was the word "sexsin." (It was actually two words.) Seated beside him on the train, Corrie did what came naturally to her—she asked her father about it.

"Father," she said, "what is sexsin?"

After sitting there quietly for a moment, Casper stood up, took hold of his heavy traveling case that was crammed with watches and other items, and set it on the floor.

"Will you carry it off the train, Corrie?"

"It's too heavy," his trusting daughter replied.

"Yes," he agreed. "And it would be a pretty poor father who would ask his little girl to carry such a load. It's the same way, Corrie, with knowledge. Some knowledge is too heavy for children. When you are older and stronger you can bear it. For now you must trust me to carry it for you."

And she did.[20] One day she would be strong enough spiritually, by the grace of God, to carry some very heavy knowledge indeed.

Another scene from Corrie's childhood: When her mother was bringing a basket of fresh bread to a family whose infant had died the night before, Corrie and Nollie went with her. As the adults in the tiny apartment spoke quietly, Nollie stood near the crib and touched the deceased baby's white cheek. Corrie hesitated for a while, but her curiosity finally won out. She reached out and touched the tiny fingers. They were stone cold, and Corrie felt a chill in her soul.

That night, she didn't eat her dinner, and then the solemn little girl went to bed. When Casper came, as was his custom, to tuck her in, Corrie cried out through sudden tears, "I need you! You can't die! You can't!"

Her father said gently, "Corrie, when you and I go to Amsterdam—when do I give you your ticket?"

"Why," his daughter sniffed, "just before we get on the train."

"Exactly," Casper replied. "And our wise Father in heaven knows when we're going to need things, too. Don't run out ahead of Him, Corrie. When the time comes that some of us will have to die, you will look into your heart and find the strength you need—just in time."[21]

When Corrie was twenty-one, she fell in love with Willem's friend Karel, twenty-six, who also was studying for the ministry. Corrie, by her own account, was a smart and practical girl, but not beautiful by the world's standards. Karel was drawn to her nonetheless, and for a season they enjoyed long walks together, and even longer conversations.

But Willem warned his little sister that Karel had been leading her on and would eventually choose someone else out of deference to his parents, who demanded that he "marry well." She tried for a time to ignore her brother's words, but the truth came out one evening when Karel showed up at the Beje with his fiancée, left unnamed in *The Hiding Place*. When the excruciating half hour was over, Corrie ran upstairs to her bedroom, where the tears could flow. She knew then that she would never marry. Soon her father was padding up after her.

"There are two things we can do when this happens," Casper told his daughter. "We can kill the love so that it stops hurting. But then part of us dies. Or, Corrie, we can ask God to open up another route for that love to travel."

"Whenever we cannot love in the old, human way, Corrie, God can give us the perfect way."[22]

God would indeed give Corrie a perfect way to share her love with those who hurt her and those she loved the most. One of those hurt loved ones was her older sister, Betsie, who in some ways is the moral center of *The Hiding Place*. Betsie, seven years older than her awestruck sister, was far prettier and more fashionable, according to Corrie. Betsie was able to take the common elements of a thrifty existence in Haarlem and transform the Beje into a place of beauty and rest. Elizabeth Sherrill said that she "could make a party out of three potatoes and some twice-used tea leaves."[23] But Betsie was frail all her life with what Corrie called "pernicious anemia."[24] Corrie therefore was very protective of her.

One November, when the weather was raw, Casper decided that his sickly daughter should no longer work the cash register near the front door of the Beje, which continually let in the raw air. From now on, Corrie would be up front with the customers, while Betsie would cook the meals and make the house a home.

Betsie, Corrie knew, was nonpareil in caring for each person who stepped into the shop. She was not, however, nearly as gifted in accounting, and their father—though a skilled watchmaker—had little idea what he was charging customers and if the accounts were up to date. Corrie therefore set her careful and exacting mind to getting the books in order. Soon she wanted to work on the watches and discovered her own gift of careful craftsmanship.

Three years after the centennial celebration of the business, only Casper, Betsie, and Corrie remained in the house, although visitors and those down on their luck were never turned away. As Adolf Hitler consolidated power, however, Holland's clouds of worry over Germany were transformed into torrents of fear. On May 10, 1940, the Nazis invaded, dropping bombs in the middle of the night.

While their aged father peacefully slept, Corrie and her older sister prayed in the front room, while repeated flashes of war gave the scene an eerie light. Kneeling by the piano bench, these two patriotic, middle-aged Dutch women prayed for their country, for those wounded or killed, and for Queen Wilhelmina. Then Betsie started praying for the Germans caught up in the rising tide of Hitler's evil. Corrie looked at her sister in the intermittent darkness.

"Oh Lord," she prayed quietly, "listen to Betsie, not me, because I cannot pray for those men at all."[25]

The ten Booms' response to this evil would be anything but passive. Holland, which had hoped to remain neutral, fell to the Nazi blitzkrieg in only five days, the queen departing as a refugee. Still, the watch shop made a lot of money during the first year of occupation, as customers bought out their stock. Ration cards were distributed, a curfew was announced, identity cards were issued, and radios were confiscated (the ten Booms gave one up and kept the other, hidden under a curve in the stairs). Order was maintained.

Soon enough, however, Holland's anti-Semites became emboldened, and their numbers grew. A rock went crashing through the window of a Jewish-owned store here; a "No Jews" sign went up there. Yellow stars were sewn to the fronts of shirts and jackets. A synagogue was razed, and the fire trucks worked not to save it but to keep the flames from spreading to other buildings. Willem, Corrie had heard, had started hiding Jewish people from the Nazis.

He was far from alone. Many German Jews, including Anne Frank, had fled to Holland during the thirties to avoid Nazi persecution. The Netherlands was well-known as a haven for the persecuted. It would not remain so during the war. According to *Christianity Today*, "At the beginning of the war, 140,000 Jews resided in the Netherlands. By its end, 107,000 (76 percent) had been deported to concentration camps or otherwise killed. Only about 5,000 survived in the general population, while another 30,000 survived by hiding or other means."[26]

During one roundup of what appeared to be a Jewish family, all wearing yellow stars, at the local Grote Markt, Corrie exclaimed, "Father! Those poor people!"

"Those poor people," Casper replied. "I pity the poor Germans, Corrie. They have touched the apple of God's eye."[27]

The decision to actively resist the evil moved a step closer when German soldiers came to loot Weil's Furriers, right across the street. Corrie urged the old Jewish owner to come inside the Beje, where he would be safe. Willem would somehow find a place for Weil and his wife, who was in Amsterdam. That night, Corrie's nephew Kik took Weil to safety. Two weeks later, Corrie saw Kik again and asked what had happened.

"If you're going to work with the underground, Tante Corrie," he said with a smile, "you must learn not to ask questions."[28] Corrie wondered whether Christians were permitted by God to lie, steal, even murder to save the Jews.

One day on their daily walk, Corrie and her now-frail father came across a man they had affectionately called the Bulldog because of his stocky frame and his habit of walking his pet bulldogs. His name, they learned upon introducing themselves, was Harry de Vries, and he was forlorn and alone.

What had happened to his dogs? Harry had poisoned them, afraid no one would care for them when the Germans came for him. For his safety, they urged de Vries to come to the Beje with his wife. He declined out of concern for their safety but began visiting at night anyway. De Vries, a Jew who had become a follower of Jesus the Messiah, was taken by all the old Jewish theological tomes that a local rabbi, before he had vanished, had given Casper for safekeeping.[29]

When Corrie visited the home of a Jewish doctor one evening, she saw him put his trusting children to bed. "He went upstairs," Corrie recalled, "and I heard the slight sounds of a minute's romping, the chatter of two child-voices, and then the footstep of the doctor as he returned down the stairs." She knew the Gestapo could separate them at any moment.[30] Then and there Corrie made up her mind, praying silently, *Lord Jesus, I offer myself for your people. In any way. Any place. Any time.*[31] Once made, the decision to defy the Nazis and protect the Jews led naturally to action for the family at Barteljorisstraat 19.

In May 1942, just before the 8:00 P.M. curfew, a woman knocked at the door, asking to come in. She had heard that the ten Booms had befriended a man on the street. "My name is Kleermaker," she said. "I'm a Jew." After she had been served some tea, she said she was afraid to return to her apartment.

"In this household," Casper said, "God's people are always welcome."[32]

Two nights later, an elderly couple knocked at the door, seeking refuge. Corrie asked her brother, Willem, to find them places and ration cards, but he said he was being watched. She would have to develop her own "sources." So Corrie, ever practical, arranged with a friend to have some ration cards stolen, and a continuing ruse to have them replenished was worked out.

Soon Corrie was ushered into the presence of a group of Dutch underground leaders. They would send a man to construct a hiding place in the Beje to protect Corrie, her houseguests, and indeed the underground movement itself from sudden raids by the Nazis. Soon a man calling himself Mr. Smit showed up, inspecting the old house's nooks and crannies. Finally, he chose Corrie's upstairs bedroom, and in six days he constructed a false wall made of brick, thirty inches from the back wall. The new wall appeared to be as old as the original, complete with water stains and built-in bookshelves. The entrance was a sliding panel, two by two, beneath the bottom shelf on the left.[33]

The hiding place was ready. Soon the ten Booms took one Jew and then another and then another into their care. Their guests, seeking food and shelter, found much more at Barteljorisstraat 19. For nearly two years they benefited from the nightly prayers and readings of Scripture, the friendship offered, the trust in God displayed. At least eighty Jews were transited through the ten Boom house to various places of safety during those two years,[34] with a small core group living there more or less permanently.

Yet Corrie and Betsie rightly feared that the Nazis were closing in. The family, with help from the underground, held one drill after another to train its guests to quickly and quietly get into the hiding place when the long-anticipated knock at the door came. One night, on February 28, 1944, it did.

Four Jews and two underground workers were there when the soldiers arrived, tipped off by an informant, and began tearing the Beje apart. So were Corrie, Betsie, Casper, Willem, Nollie, and Nollie's son, Peter (who had already spent time in prison for playing the Dutch national anthem during a church service in Velsen). The four Jewish guests and their two helpers scrambled into the hiding place upstairs, undetected. They remained inside for two days before the underground rescued them.

For Corrie's family, however, the trial was just beginning. They were taken to nearby Scheveningen Prison and processed. A Gestapo officer offered to send Casper home if he promised not to "cause any more trouble." The old man replied, "If I go home today, I will open my door again to any man in need who knocks."[35] He would die in custody, separated from his daughters, not much more than a week later, at the age of eighty-four.

Corrie and Betsie were transported to Vught Concentration Camp in June. In September, the two were crammed into a boxcar, transported to the notorious Ravensbrück Concentration Camp for women, where some prisoners were subjected to forced labor, participation in SS-enforced brothels, unethical medical experimentation, and execution.[36] In all, an estimated ninety-six thousand women perished there.[37]

During the ordeal, Corrie came to see that God is her hiding place no matter what, and that, when all that she loves is taken from her, love remains. While Betsie lay on a stretcher in the camp medical ward shortly before her death, her words to Corrie would keep her little sister steady and provide hope when all hope seemed lost: "There is no pit so deep that He is not deeper still."[38]

It is a message that Corrie ten Boom would share with the world.

CHAPTER 4

A COMMUNICATOR
IS BORN

Haarlem wasn't the only European city where two Christian women prayed during a bombing attack. On the night of September 11, 1944, over the southern German city of Darmstadt, the No. 5 Group of the Royal Air Force leveled the city, making 66,000 of the city's 110,000 residents homeless overnight.[1]

That night Klara Schlink and Erika Madauss "found themselves vividly confronted with their own mortality," says historian George Faithful of Dominican University of California.[2] "In their prayers that night they committed their lives completely to God." The next morning, these women, who were leaders of a Bible study in the Lutheran Church, found themselves among the survivors in the devastated city.[3]

More than their possible deaths had been on these women's minds. According to Faithful, "[They] had always fought against the teachings of the *Reich Church*, emphasizing continuity between the Old and New Testaments, and the special status of the Jews as God's chosen people. They also incorporated intense supernaturalism into their teaching, in contrast to the prevailing rationalism of German theology."[4]

True to their promise, after the war was finally over, in September 1947, Schlink and Madauss formally founded the

Evangelical Sisterhood of Mary. From then on, Schlink would be known as Mother Basilea and Madauss would be Mother Martyria. The new order of Protestant nuns embraced poverty, celibacy, and communal, cloistered life.

Mother Basilea, the spiritual and intellectual leader of the Evangelical Sisterhood of Mary, emphasized both repentance and Jewish-Christian reconciliation. Summarizing her thought, Faithful writes, "The German people bore a collective debt to the Jewish people. German Christians were complicit in the Holocaust because of their overwhelming silence. They had a special duty to repent of the war and to seek reconciliation with Jews and with the new nation of Israel. Even when it was near impossible for a German citizen to secure a visa to travel there, Mother Basilea went to Israel, establishing a home to care for Holocaust survivors."[5]

In 1966, the sisters completed the construction of their cloister, which is called *Kanaan*. The first building, called the Motherhouse, was built with stones from a demolished Nazi army barracks. An anonymous sister said that "everything here should be a reminder of the great Canaan, the Holy Land, and, with it, Jesus."[6]

In May 1968, Elizabeth Sherrill visited *Kanaan*, which continued the sisterhood's work of assisting Jewish survivors, letting them tell their stories, and speaking the truth about the Nazi era.[7] Sherrill was drawn there because the cloister and its work stood in such contrast to the anti-Semitism and outright Holocaust denial she was hearing. Sherrill, who was born in 1928, said the war was "terribly real" to her during her high school years in Scarsdale, New York. She wanted people to remember what happened so that such horrors would never happen again.[8]

"At that point, there was an effort to sweep it under the rug," Sherrill recalled. "Most Germans were in denial and went to great

Elizabeth Sherrill said that Corrie had the skills of an actress.
"She could put on a face like someone just in from the potato fields.
She could have gotten away with anything."

lengths thinking the Holocaust never happened. It was simply too terrible to believe."[9]

Sherrill and her husband, John, were also in the early stages of founding a new publishing house, called Chosen Books. Their goal was to search "the world for books that would have two criteria. They would be interesting. They would be helpful."[10] The couple was also looking to develop new authors. Sherrill stumbled upon both at *Kanaan.*

Two speakers were featured during an evening service. One was a Jewish man who had survived brutal treatment at a concentration camp; his father and brother had not. The man was shaking and bitter, still traumatized. Then the other speaker stood up—white-haired and wearing sensible shoes. Though this woman, too, had lost numerous loved ones to the Nazi horror and had seen the worst evil that human nature can inflict, she was beaming with peace and joy.

"I want to talk with you," Elizabeth Sherrill said when the talk was over. "You must have some secret."[11]

Indeed she did. In the camps she had found a "hiding place from the wind, and a covert from the tempest . . . the shadow of a great rock in a weary land" (Isa. 32:2).[12] The woman's name was Corrie ten Boom.

Of course, her ten months as a prisoner of the Nazis in 1944 weren't the only source of her peace and poise that night. Corrie always had been a doer, as shown by her many quiet years between the wars of ministering to boys and girls during difficult economic times. These ministries also helped her to begin honing her gifts as a communicator. By her own account, Corrie even evangelized the mentally challenged in Haarlem. Later she would tell a Gestapo officer in Scheveningen Prison, Lieutenant Rahms, "The Bible reveals [the Lord Jesus] as One who has great love and mercy for all who are small and weak and poor. It is possible that in His sight a mentally deficient person is of greater worth than you or I."[13]

Pamela Rosewell Moore, a British woman who served with Brother Andrew's mission from 1968 to 1976 and as Corrie's personal assistant from 1976 until her death in 1983, says that Corrie and Betsie started a group to "teach the girls the Gospel and keep them off the streets." Each week the girls, who were in their early teens, were expected to present a story from the Bible while their peers offered critiques. They were expected to address the following kinds of questions:

> Was the Gospel clear?
> How was her first sentence? Did it attract attention?
> Was there humor?
> What help was offered for the girls this week?
> What importance did the story have for eternity?

Did she describe colors, movements?

Did she draw clear pictures with good illustrations?

Was it an inspiration for action, for faith, for endurance?[14]

Under Corrie's leadership, these clubs grew into the Triangle Girls movement, which Moore describes as "a Christian Girl Scout movement." Some of the girls who joined were physically disabled. One girl, named Kitty, said of her experience:

> At the camps we had a campfire and each evening we always paid good attention to what Tante Corrie said in her talks. Her simple way of telling things made a deep impression on me and many others. And she always gave us something to think about after the talk ended. I always listened closely, looking at her beautiful, friendly eyes, which spoke so much love to us. Tante Corrie was a wonderful pedagogue. And she had such a great sense of humor that I can hardly describe it. She laid in my heart the basis of faith.[15]

Elizabeth Sherrill would later say that Corrie had the skills of an actress. "She could put on a face like someone just in from the potato fields," Sherrill said. "She could have gotten away with anything. She had different personae for different situations."[16] Corrie was especially persuasive in her native Dutch. "She was a machine when she spoke in Dutch," Sherrill said. "She had them pinned to the back of their chairs when preaching hell and damnation."

After the war, Corrie put her communication gifts to good use, to say the least. After returning to Holland, she continued to wake up early, as if she were preparing for morning roll call in Ravensbrück. Not wanting to waste her time, Corrie instead started writing about her experiences. The result was her first book, *Gevangene en Toch*, *A Prisoner and Yet . . .* , amazingly, published in 1945.[17] This book chronicles Corrie's first-person recollections of the Beje, Scheveningen, Vught, Ravensbrück, and the early days after her release. It would be translated into English in 1954, as Corrie's ministry grew.

All this was just part of a speaking itinerary to rival, and perhaps exceed, the apostle Paul's. At first, she spoke with friends and neighbors, traveling to the various venues on her bicycle. When one lady told Corrie kindly that her faith must have brought her through, Corrie gave her Lord the credit, replying, "No, it was Jesus! . . . You can trust that He who helped me through will do the same for you. I have always believed it, but now I know from my own experience that His light is stronger than the deepest darkness."[18]

This settled conviction about the personal care of her Savior impelled Corrie to share her message in ever wider circles in Holland and, soon, around the world. After setting up a rehabilitation center in a donated mansion in the seaside resort town of Bloemendaal for those who had suffered mental and physical anguish during the war, Corrie soon was headed to America on a cargo ship, with fifty dollars in her pocket. Her first audience was a group of Christian Jews who had emigrated to New York City. Her message was in German.[19]

In *Life Lessons from the Hiding Place*, Moore describes Corrie's thickly packed schedule as the ministry grew. Much of it was centered in the United States and Canada. In the coming years, she would also work in Germany, England, Bermuda, and Japan. At this point, Corrie was sixty years old. Though she had always been physically stronger than Betsie, Corrie had to cope with a variety of ailments while maintaining her sometimes-exhausting schedule. Where did she get such energy for ministry and holy wanderlust?

Tante Jans, Corrie's mother's sister, may provide a clue. Jans, a Christian author and activist, came to live at the Beje in 1895 until her death from diabetes in 1919 at the age of seventy-one. Jans, Corrie remembered, took the two second-story rooms of the front house, above the shop. In the first "she wrote the flaming Christian tracts for which she was known all over Holland."

Corrie added that Jans "believed that our welfare in the hereafter depended on how much we could accomplish here on earth."[20] At the outset of the Great War, right after her diagnosis, Corrie said, Jans "threw herself more forcefully than ever into writing, speaking, forming clubs, and launching projects." One was a soldiers' center in Haarlem, a novel idea at the time.[21]

Diabetes was a death sentence in those days, and one day the family had to tell Jans that she had three weeks to live. But Casper tried to comfort Jans with the thought that she would be able to bring her many accomplishments to God. They were all shocked when, in tears, the sickly woman replied, "What does He care for our little tricks and trinkets?" Then she whispered in prayer, "Dear Jesus, I thank you that we must come to you with empty hands. I thank you that you have done all—all—on the cross, and that all we need in life or death is to be sure of this."[22]

Jans would stand before God with empty hands, as we all must do, but they were never idle. Neither were Corrie's.

After the war, Corrie shared the Gospel at a prison in Darmstadt holding women who had been guards at Ravensbrück.[23] Corrie, though very intelligent, was not getting through to these women, who considered her approach theologically unsophisticated. So she prayed to God for guidance, and the word *chocolate* came to her. When she returned to the prison for a final visit, Corrie shared the chocolate she had brought along. The inmates' faces lit up with gratitude. Chocolate was an extravagance they had not enjoyed in a long time. Some even asked Corrie for her name and address.

"No one questioned me about this chocolate," Corrie told them. "No one asked whether it had been manufactured in Holland or what quantities it contained of cocoa, sugar, milk, or vitamins. You have done exactly what I intended you to do; you have eaten and enjoyed it."

Then she went on, holding her Bible high: "It is just the same with this Book. If I read about the Bible in a scientific, theological, or scholarly way, it does not make me happy. But if I read that God so loved the world that He gave His only begotten Son, that whoever (and this means Corrie ten Boom also) believes in Him, should not perish but have eternal life (see John 3:16), then I am really happy."

She met one of these women, months later, dying in a German hospital. "Last year I was a prisoner in Darmstadt," she said. "When you visited the camp, you preached on chocolate. That was the moment of my conversion."

As the 1950s unfolded, Corrie's speaking took her to Taiwan, New Zealand, Israel, South Africa, Spain, Switzerland, and Holland. A second book, *Amazing Love*, was published in 1953. Over the next several years she spoke in the United States, Canada, New Mexico, New Zealand, India, Borneo, and Formosa. In 1954, her experience of God deepened as she received what is called the baptism of the Holy Spirit. In nearly four decades of ministry, Corrie would travel to sixty-three countries—many of them more than once.

In 1956 Corrie finally met Wilhelmina, who by this time had abdicated the throne to her daughter, becoming *Princess Wilhelmina*. "Princess Wilhelmina knew her Bible very well, and we enjoyed those hours in her lovely private chamber," Corrie later wrote. "She gave me the opportunity to tell her of the miracle God had worked in my life to forgive my enemies."[24] Several years later, Corrie would be named a knight in the Order Orange-Nassau by Queen Juliana.

In India, in 1958, Corrie was rebaptized (by immersion) at the William Carey Baptist Church in Calcutta by the pastor, Walter A. Corlett, who founded the Calcutta Bible College in 1955.[25] The church was founded on January 1, 1809, by the Protestant missionary pioneers William Carey, Joshua Marshman, and William Ward.[26] Corrie, who had been christened as an infant in the Dutch Reformed Church, was characteristically blunt about her ecclesiastical shift, saying that her baptism in the small Calcutta church was more biblical than sprinkling.[27]

The next year, Corrie visited Ravensbrück, where she discovered that her release came "accidentally," via a clerical error. All other women her age had been murdered by the Nazis prior to the Allied liberation of the camp.

Separately about this time, another Hollander, Brother Andrew, was beginning his Bible-smuggling ministry to persecuted Christians in the Soviet bloc. *Christianity Today* reported that Andrew, who was born in 1928, and Corrie first met while working together in the Dutch resistance during World War II, when he was still a teenager.[28] Their association grew until her death in 1983. In a memorial tribute to Corrie, Andrew said that they became friends while writing for the same Dutch magazine, *Power from on High*.[29]

In 1966, Andrew and Corrie separately went to the Berlin Congress on Evangelism convened by Billy Graham—he as a participant and she as a speaker. Andrew was traveling with the Sherrills. He marveled at Corrie's ability even then to connect with all kinds of people, no matter how august or learned.

There was a printed booklet with the names of all the speakers. Some speakers had so many titles: Professor, Doctor, Chairman—and a whole list of their accomplishments. Honorary degrees. Earned degrees. All they'd done. Very impressive. But when they spoke, nobody listened because all the speeches were printed in our program. You could just sit there and instead of simultaneous translation, you could just read if you want[ed], or take a nap. But then you turn the page and you saw "Speaker, Corrie ten Boom. Occupation, Watchmaker." Nothing more. It was such a contrast, almost ridiculous. Yet wherever you went that week, four or five days, in that huge building in West Berlin, wherever you saw a group of people around a person, it was always around Corrie. Whenever she was spotted, people would gather around her and ask questions or she would pray with them. None of the other speakers had any visible following. Corrie sure had.[30]

In 1967, the two shared ministry in Vietnam, during the war. Details are sketchy, but one biographer says that she was close enough to the fighting to hear bullets zipping through the foliage as she traveled by jeep to share the gospel with soldiers. Andrew, according to this source, was teaching the gospel and ransoming Vietnamese children sold into slavery.[31] Later, Andrew would serve on the boards of both her Dutch and American foundations,[32] until her death in 1983.

Corrie was not only an inspirational speaker; she was a learner. In 1962, at the age of seventy, she and her then-companion, Conny van Hoogstraten, were incognito counselors at the Billy Graham crusade at Chicago's Soldier Field, where the great evangelist asked a throng of 116,000 people, "The great question of our time is, will we be motivated by materialistic philosophy or by spiritual power?"[33] Corrie told her supporters, "Conny and I both studied the training course for counselors, and like the other 4,000 counselors we worked as much as possible after the meetings in the inquiry rooms. We learned much, also for the future."[34]

The gift of connecting with her audience, whether it was sophisticated or simple, remained with Corrie throughout the decades of her life. Moore tells of her first encounter with Corrie, while she was attending a mission conference in 1968 in north-central England for English and Dutch youths: "When Corrie's turn came to speak, my first impression of this thoroughly Dutch lady was that at 76 years of age she looked strong, of sturdy build, and possessed a chin that can be well-described as determined. And characteristic of the Dutch, her conference messages were delivered with no sentiment or emotionalism. 'There is no pit so deep, the love of God is not deeper still,' she said, speaking of her imprisonment in concentration camp."[35]

So did Corrie's ability remain, with the Lord's help, to forgive those who had harmed her. She told the following now-famous story of meeting a former SS officer from Ravensbrück—who had stood guard at the shower room—after she spoke at a church in Munich in 1947:

> He was the first of our actual jailers that I had seen since that time. . . .
>
> He came up to me as the church was emptying, beaming and bowing. "How grateful I am for your message, *Fraulein*," he said. "To think that, as you say, He has washed my sins away!"

His hand was thrust out to shake mine. And I, who had preached so often to the people in Bloemendaal the need to forgive, kept my hand at my side.

Even as the angry, vengeful thoughts boiled through me, I saw the sin of them. . . . *Lord Jesus, I prayed, forgive me and help me to forgive him.*

I tried to smile, I struggled to raise my hand. I could not. And so again I breathed a silent prayer. *Jesus, I cannot forgive him. Give Your forgiveness.*

As I took his hand the most incredible thing happened. From my shoulder along my arm and through my hand, a current seemed to pass from me to him, while into my heart sprang a love for this stranger that almost overwhelmed me.[36]

In that moment Corrie ten Boom, a middle-aged survivor of Nazi terror, confronted the darkness in her own soul in a way she never had before. And in that moment, crying out for God's grace, she experienced the paradoxical triumph of Jesus the Victor, the Savior who died and rose again. Corrie was victorious.

CHAPTER 5

A STORY
IS RETOLD

John and Elizabeth Sherrill met as college students in 1947 aboard a ship while traveling to Switzerland to continue their studies. John had served in the US Army during the Allied invasion of Italy. They would have been married for seventy years if not for John's death at the age of ninety-four in December 2017. In 1952, John became an associate editor at *Guideposts*. He had a heart for people of all kinds and an eye for detail.

Elizabeth told a story about a family reunion when John mentioned someone named Gladys. "Gladys?" people asked. "Who's Gladys?" John replied, "The one with three children, the oldest who is going to college. She works at the checkout."[1]

The Sherrills were always sniffing around for a story. Rick Hamlin, *Guideposts* executive editor, says the couple frequently haunted the offices of local newspapers in search of writing fodder. "When *Guideposts* launched its Writers Workshops in 1967," Hamlin said, "John and Elizabeth were crucial teachers and led those workshops and many others over the decades. He often stressed the importance of vivid scenes and dramatic storytelling and was a guide and inspiration for many as they launched their writing careers."[2]

Elizabeth continues to share her late husband's passion for *the story*. She said in an interview that books about Corrie "became a kind of industry," adding, "I don't know why people don't go out and find their own stories. There are so many stories out there. What is lacking is a writer who will tell someone *else's* story."[3]

When Elizabeth heard Corrie that night in 1968, she knew she had a *story* and quickly convinced Corrie to write another book about her experiences. Surprisingly, Elizabeth had to work harder to convince her husband to support the new project for Chosen Books. It was the first time she had agreed to do a book without his approval.

"I came home and told John about the book agreement," she said. "He was appalled, saying, 'A Dutch spinster? A watchmaker? Readers are very America-centered. No one's interested in books about World War II.'"[4]

Like publishers the world over, John would not take a story, however good or inspiring, if he didn't think it would *sell*. Such hardheaded realism helps keep publishers in business. For once, however, John Sherrill was wrong—*dead* wrong—about the marketability of this story, even though Corrie was not a big name.

"At the time she and I met in Darmstadt," Elizabeth Sherrill said, "she was known to the Holocaust survivors she ministered to, and anywhere she could find an audience for her message of forgiveness. She especially liked to address former Nazis—though of course at that time most Germans were in denial that death camps had ever existed."[5]

Because of her enthusiasm for this book, Elizabeth would be the main writer. John's main role would be as publisher. Pamela Rosewell Moore, however, says that John's contributions as an author were significant, particularly in the caring way he interviewed Corrie. "I'm in awe of him," Moore said. "All the way through [the book] you can see his kindness and thoroughness."[6]

In the almost fifty years since *The Hiding Place* was first published, a story has made the rounds that the Sherrills learned of Corrie's story through Brother Andrew, the Bible smuggler from the Netherlands.[7] (John and Elizabeth had helped Andrew write his story in the 1967 page-turner, *God's Smuggler.*) Elizabeth Sherrill insists this is not the case.

"Brother Andrew never mentioned Corrie to me," Elizabeth said. "It was she who told me that they knew each other—indeed had traveled together."[8] As a matter of fact, Corrie surprised her at their first meeting, saying, "You wrote a book for my friend, Anne van der Bijl."[9] (Andrew's friends called him by the nickname "Anne.")

Still, the Sherrills' prior friendship with Andrew no doubt gave John and Elizabeth (Tibby to her friends and loved ones) a head start on what would prove to be a challenging, time-consuming project. Andrew could instruct this couple, who would go on to sell more than fifty million books in their long publishing careers, on Dutch culture, on Corrie, and on ministry in difficult places.

But their main source about what happened, and how to tell it, would of course be Corrie. But despite the fact that this woman, now well into her seventies, was a powerful communicator to all kinds of audiences, she was somewhat below that standard when talking with Elizabeth about her life. As the writing was being finished, Corrie told supporters that "the enemy brought all kinds of difficulties along."[10]

She also said, "It is very hard for Tibby to write these last chapters; she is living what she describes. This is why this last part of the book is such a great strain for John and Tibby Sherrill. Thank you for your prayers for them. I believe that this book will be a great blessing for many people, and I am sure that the Lord will use it to reach many more than my other books have done. The name of the Lord will be glorified."[11]

Some of the difficulties that Corrie, John, and Elizabeth experienced also were no doubt the garden-variety struggles that most writers experience from time to time. When Elizabeth first started talking with Corrie about her family, she struggled with how to tell the story of this hero of the Dutch underground in a realistic, believable way. Compelling narratives require tension and conflict as they explore characters and move toward a dramatic conclusion. In itself, Corrie's experience at the Beje, with its close-knit family and profound influence of faith in the Lord, while a blessing to all involved, provided very little narrative opportunity. As J. R. R. Tolkien once wrote, "Now it is a strange thing, but things that are good to have and days that are good to spend are soon told about, and not much to listen to; while things that are uncomfortable, palpitating, and even gruesome, may make a good tale, and take a deal of telling anyway."[12] Elizabeth knew all this and struggled to find a way to humanize Corrie so that readers would be able to identify with her as a fellow struggler.

But as they talked, Elizabeth started to hear of some of the family tensions: the self-assured pushiness of Tante Jans, the complaining of Tante Bep. Then she learned how Corrie often felt in awe of her father and Betsie on a spiritual level. While they consistently expressed faith in God, whatever the circumstances, Corrie was slower to absorb such spiritual lessons.

"When Corrie began to talk about Betsie," Elizabeth recalled, "I said, 'Aha! I have it—that's my way in!'" In *The Hiding Place*, Corrie would be cast as "the learner"; Casper and Betsie would be "the wise ones."[13] Corrie's readers would learn right alongside her.

Elizabeth, a journalist, wanted concrete details—how people looked, what color an object was, what a certain food tasted like, what Corrie heard during a particular incident. These were details, however, that mattered little to Corrie, who was much more concerned about someone's character or relationship with God than with the kind of shoes he or she wore. Yet such details are the stuff of journalistic verisimilitude.

"It was done almost in blood," Elizabeth recalled. "It took the two of us backing her into a corner."[14] She added on her website:

> What was it like to work with Corrie ten Boom? Like trying to get a blind man to describe the colors of a garden he'd once walked in. "Corrie," I would say, "describe Mr. Koornstra who got you those extra ration cards."
>
> "He was a very brave man."
>
> "I know. But what did he look like? Was he tall? Short? Thin—fat? Bald? Did he have a beard?"
>
> And with that tone of finality that only Dutch-accented English can convey: "He was a *man*."
>
> It was that way with clothing, streets, houses. I remember my mental image of the Beje, the family home which became "the hiding place," before I went to Haarlem and saw it for myself. "It was a small house!" Corrie kept saying—clearly pleased to provide this physical detail, since I seemed so keen on them.
>
> But as I tried to envisage the various floors—a short stairway from her bedroom down to a hallway where there were four more bedrooms, down again to her parents' bedroom, a long staircase down to the dining room, another to the back door, a "few steps" up from the dining room to "the front rooms"—I was picturing an American-style split-level, growing ever larger as the room-count reached thirteen. A detail Corrie never mentioned was that the house was only one room wide.
>
> Day after day the annoying questions continued. How high, how wide, how old, what color, what did

it sound like, how did it taste. "What does it matter?" Corrie would demand after failing once more to recall a single specific about a dress she'd worn or a prison cell where she'd been held.

"It doesn't matter," I'd agree, "in the working out of God's purposes for mankind. But it matters for the paragraph I'm working on."[15]

Pam Moore had a slightly different take on Corrie's forgetfulness. The book would require that Corrie and Elizabeth travel to the Netherlands and elsewhere to flesh out some of the details—to visit the Beje and the camps, to study old photos and documents, and to interview living witnesses, such as Meyer Mossell (Eusie in the book) and Corrie's nephew Peter.

Moore was a missionary helper to Brother Andrew, who was present during some of the writing sessions in the Netherlands in 1968. Andrew had volunteered her to transcribe the hours of tape-recorded interviews between Corrie and the Sherrills.[16] According to Moore, the problem wasn't just that Corrie couldn't recall the details, although a fuzzy recall was at least part of the problem. It was that she was "at first unwilling to unlock memories of her wartime experiences,"[17] at least from the camps. With prodding, however, some of even those dark memories returned.

"During the coming months of the writing of the book," Moore recalled, "she made herself remember. I transcribed many tapes, and . . . it was fascinating to see the . . . skillful blending of such details as soldiers and trees with the element of danger for the ten Boom family."[18]

Elizabeth Sherrill said Corrie was the kind of spiritual person for whom such details didn't matter. "Their minds are on higher things," Sherrill said. "It wasn't that she was being stingy with her recollections. She didn't notice."[19]

The differences in scope and style between Corrie's first attempt to convey her experiences, *A Prisoner and Yet . . .* , and the professionally researched and written *The Hiding Place* are notable. The former account drops readers right into the wartime ten Boom house, which is described as "the gayest underground address in the Netherlands."[20] The "curiously constructed"[21] house is described as small but, in contrast to Elizabeth Sherrill's painstaking research, no details are provided. The physical hiding place for Jewish guests and underground workers is called the "angelcrib," an unexplained term nowhere present in *The Hiding Place*.

In *A Prisoner and Yet . . .* , we know little about the ten Boom family, other than its love for the Jews, though its motivations are largely unexplored. Casper is almost a peripheral figure, a kind but somewhat confused old man rather than the spiritual patriarch as he is portrayed in *The Hiding Place*. Nollie is not named at all. Difficult terms are explained in notes at the back of the book. *A Prisoner and Yet . . .* covers much of the same ground as the 1971 bestseller, but the events are told two-dimensionally. Transitions are abrupt, explanations few. Spiritual lessons, however, are sprinkled liberally throughout the oft-grim narrative, making the parts feel somehow mismatched.

In contrast, the Sherrills positioned *The Hiding Place*, which carried a price tag of $5.95, as an adventure story. "Here is Corrie ten Boom's story," they said, "for the vast number of people who have loved her devotional writings and talks. This book is also for anyone, for that matter, who loves rousing adventure."[22]

Elizabeth Sherrill says such a broad focus was deliberate. "We never wrote for an audience," she said. "We always wrote for a person."[23] With *God's Smuggler*, they imagined communicating with a teenager "who thought church was boring." For *The*

Hiding Place, the pictured reader was "a middle-aged man bored with religious lingo, whose wife would slip him little Christian tracts in the hope they would take."[24] Elizabeth says sometimes she would clip a picture from a magazine that reminded her of the imaginary reader and would then ask, "Am I reaching you?"[25] Promotional copy highlighted the hortatory aim of the book, as a spiritual primer for life in a difficult world.

> It was not the sites visited, nor the towering adventure, that demanded this book to be written. It was the lessons they learned, the lessons in daily living, intensely practical ones that will be prized by all Christians, facing the uncertainties we are living in now, in the seventies. "The Hiding Place" is a book as powerful as the other Sherrill successes: "The Cross and the Switchblade," "God's Smuggler," "They Speak with Other Tongues."[26]

Upon the November 8, 1971, publication of *The Hiding Place*, Corrie thanked her supporters. "Without your prayers," she wrote, "it would have been impossible for John and Tibby Sherrill to accomplish such a tremendous work. They both are beautiful tools in God's hands."

"I myself had much joy to read it," Corrie continued in her slightly stilted English. "I saw myself walking again through the streets of Haarlem, and sitting around the table with our big 'family.'"[27]

So would millions of readers.

CHAPTER 6

—

ANNE
AND CORRIE

The Hiding Place was a huge hit, selling millions of copies and bringing Corrie ten Boom to an almost stratospheric level of evangelical celebrity. Larry Eskridge, the historian of American evangelicalism, said the book followed a well-worn path. "*The Hiding Place* fits into a long-established genre of 'Christian Hero' books," Eskridge said. "The earliest such were, of course, biographies [such as Jonathan] Edwards' [*The Life and Diary of*] *David Brainerd* and books about other missionaries, famous evangelists, and Christian workers, which were a staple right up through World War II. These books continued to be important on down into the 21st-century, although their scope broadened— think *Born Again*, *The Chaplain of Bourbon Street*, *Daktar*, *Turned on to Jesus*, and on and on."[1]

Yet Eskridge praised the book's fresh approach, which he called "a particularly appealing spin on the . . . genre—similar in many ways to the Sherrills' earlier book *God's Smuggler*—with its tension and excitement, its focus on events many readers had lived through, its story about a true layperson—a woman!—and a context that was not directly tied into conventional narratives of amazing evangelistic triumphs or pioneering missions work."

Eskridge even wondered whether *The Hiding Place* could be called "the uplifting evangelical equivalent" to *Anne Frank: The Diary of a Young Girl*.[2] Anne Frank, of course, was a German Jew who went into hiding with her family and three other Jewish people, including a boy named Peter. For two long and confined years, these eight Jews lived in a secret wing of an Amsterdam office building during the Nazi occupation. It is during this time that the ten Boom family also began working with the Dutch resistance and hiding Jews at the Beje in Haarlem.

Anne kept a diary to record her observations about her growth into young womanhood, about her family, and, incidentally but poignantly, about trying to live an ordinary life under the constant threat of exposure and death. In her diary, the precocious and beautiful girl rarely commented about the war or political matters. Instead, it was her girlish idealism, contrasted with readers' knowledge of her coming betrayal, capture, and death, that made her tragic story so extraordinary. In a way that few other books had done, *Anne Frank* put an innocent face on the slaughter of six million Jews.

In her diary on February 23, 1944, Anne, then fourteen, recounted a visit to the attic with her friend Peter for some fresh air through the window, where she saw the roofs of the city against a pale blue sky. She wrote, "'As long as this exists,' I thought, 'and I may live to see it, the sunshine, the cloudless skies, while this lasts, I cannot be unhappy."[3]

According to the book's afterword, the Gestapo penetrated the hiding place of the Franks and their companions on August 4, 1944. The eight were subsequently sent to Westerbork, a transit camp in the country's northeast. Then, on September 3, as Brussels fell to the Allies, the Franks were among the last thousand Jews to be shipped out of the Netherlands by the Nazis. They were jammed onto a freight train, with seventy-five people in each car. There was only one small window on each car, which was sealed shut. For three days and nights, the Franks meandered eastward across Germany. They stopped in Poland, at a camp called Auschwitz. There the men were separated from the women.

A fellow prisoner there later recounted, "I can still see her standing at the door and looking down the camp street as a herd of naked gypsy girls was driven by to the crematory, and Anne watched them go and cried. And she cried also when we marched past the Hungarian children who had already been waiting half a day in the rain in front of the gas chambers because it was not yet their turn. And Anne nudged me and said: 'Look, look. Their eyes . . .'"[4]

In October, Anne, her sister Margot, and Mrs. van Daan—one of those hiding with her in the office building—were moved along with the youngest and strongest women to Belsen, in Germany. Unlike Auschwitz, this prison lacked food and water, and typhus was ravaging the camp. The Allies were on the verge of victory, but for Anne it was too late. A witness said that sometime in March she died at Belsen "peacefully, feeling that nothing bad was happening to her."[5]

Anne's diary, sketches, and stories had been strewn all over the floor of the Franks' hiding place in Amsterdam, considered worthless by the Gestapo. At first, Anne's father, Otto Frank, who had survived his ordeal, only shared copies of the diary privately. But a Dutch university professor urged him to seek a wider audience, and in June 1947, Contact Publishers in Amsterdam released Anne's diary under the title *Het Achterbuis, The Secret Annexe*. The first print run was a very typical 4,500 copies.

Sales, however, wildly exceeded expectations. A pocket edition followed quickly. It sold 900,000 copies. The book was published in France in 1950. In 1952, England and the United States received their own version, under the title *Anne Frank: The Diary of a Young Girl*.[6] The response was electric and continues to expand. Only two decades after its initial publication, the book had been translated into thirty-one languages and sold in thirty countries. The Pocket Books edition sold nearly four million copies.

There are several striking parallels, and some important differences, between *Anne Frank: The Diary of a Young Girl* and *The Hiding Place*, both in the works themselves and in the receptions they received. First, of course, is the similarity of the original title given to Anne Frank's diary, *The Secret Annexe*, and the name of Corrie's ten Boom's iconic book, *The Hiding Place*.

When asked whether this similarity was intentional, Elizabeth Sherrill answered with a firm *no*. She said she was of course aware of *Anne Frank* but chose not to read it, as the Second World War was already too "terribly real" to her. "I've never read that diary," she said. "I knew what she'd written. I'm very empathetic and take on the feelings of people. I didn't want to expose myself to it."[7]

Nevertheless, both book titles—the original one given to Anne Frank's diary and *The Hiding Place*—suggest the idea of hiding from danger, a powerful theme for people being confronted with the unwelcome truth of evil in a chaotic world. While the small space in the back wall of Corrie's bedroom was for hiding Jews, her book ultimately reveals that her true hiding place was a God who would never fail her: "You are my hiding place and my shield; / I hope in your word" (Ps. 119:14). By contrast, Anne's hiding place, the "secret annexe," was a three-story space, entered from a landing above the Opekta company offices—a space that ultimately *did* fail her.

Another similarity in the books was the space devoted to the heroic helpers. In *Anne Frank*, Otto Frank's employees come to the rescue, supplying the Franks and the others with food, occasional gifts, and moments of much-craved companionship. Although Anne does not mention any religious motivations for their selfless and risky actions, she reports with gratitude their giving Christmas presents to those in hiding. It seems clear that they are Christians sent to love and protect their Jewish friends and colleagues. *The Hiding Place*, of course, is replete with the Christian motivations of Corrie and her fellow rescuers.

The timelines of hiding, capture, and imprisonment are similar in both books. Corrie started working with the resistance to hide Jews in Haarlem in the early spring of 1942. The Franks went into hiding in Amsterdam that July. The ten Booms were betrayed by an informant and arrested by the Gestapo in February 1944. The Franks were betrayed, discovered, and arrested that August. Corrie and Betsie were shipped by train to Vught in June, then on to Ravensbrück in August. In September, Anne was among the last group of Jews sent out of Holland, by train, to Auschwitz. In October, she was sent to Belsen. In December, Betsie died at Ravensbrück, while Corrie was released. Anne died at Belsen, probably in March.

The differences in atmosphere between the two hiding places are occasionally stark. While Corrie and the Sherrills report sicknesses, fears, and occasional tensions, the reader gets a consistent picture of a home full of adults seeking to make the best of things, with small, classical concerts, literature readings, and other activities. Anne's diary, however, often brings out the pettiness, impatience, and bickering of people confined in close quarters for far too long. Anne's account is, understandably, seen through the often self-focused eyes of a nonreligious young teenager. Corrie's is seen through the eyes of a learning but mature Christian woman. Corrie's account is ultimately one of victory, while Anne's is ultimately one of tragedy.

Both accounts spread beyond the pages of a single book and infiltrated the popular imagination. Anne Frank's story was serialized in newspapers and magazines, memorialized in a play that received a Pulitzer Prize, and turned into a film and, later, a television program. The play premiered simultaneously in seven German cities on October 1, 1956. "Audiences there greeted it in stunned silence," the book's afterword reports. "The play released a wave of emotion that finally broke through the silence with which Germans had treated the Nazi period. For the first time there were widespread expressions of guilt and shame for what Germans had done to the Jews only a few years before."[8]

Corrie's admittedly more upbeat story also produced other works, artistic and otherwise. In Birmingham, England, an opera was performed, with the Sherrills in attendance. *The Hiding Place* is still performed as a play from time to time. Tim Gregory's adaptation of the book at Chicago's Provision Theater drew strong reviews, one critic calling it "a major theatrical achievement."[9] As with Anne Frank's *Diary*, Corrie's account is studied in schools, complete with online and published study guides for homeschools and others, discussion guides, and lesson plans. And of course there were the books she produced immediately after *The Hiding Place* (*Tramp for the Lord*, 1974; *In My Father's House*, 1974; and *Corrie ten Boom's Prison Letters*, 1975), as well as multiple volumes that came before and after.

However, the biggest cultural impact of *The Hiding Place*—one that may have reached even more people than the book itself—was not a book at all. It was the 1975 film produced by the Billy Graham Evangelistic Association.

CHAPTER 7

ON THE SILVER SCREEN

Though she was an inveterate writer, eventually publishing thirty books, Corrie's dream ever since she wrote *A Prisoner and Yet . . .* had been to turn that early book into a film. Writing for the January 1972 edition of her newsletter, *It's Harvest Time*, Corrie was frank about this goal, and blunt about why it never happened.

"Many years ago," she said, "I wrote . . . about the possibility of making a movie of my book: 'A Prisoner and Yet.' We prayed much for it, but it never happened. With 'The Hiding Place' there is better material for a movie."[1] The leaders at World Wide Pictures, the filmmaking arm of the Billy Graham Evangelistic Association, evidently agreed.

There are differing accounts of how Corrie ten Boom and Billy Graham became partners in ministry. Wheaton College's Billy Graham Center Archives says she became friends with Billy and his wife, Ruth, in 1960, adding, "This was the start of an increasingly close relationship."[2] Pam Moore agrees that they met in 1960.[3]

Gigi Graham, the evangelist's eldest daughter, was living in Switzerland at the time, married to Stephan Tchividjian, a Swiss citizen. Corrie's nephew Peter van Woerden—a son of Nollie—lived there and knew Stephan's family, who introduced Billy and

Ruth Graham to Corrie.[4] Billy Graham's 1997 autobiography, *Just as I Am*, describes the high esteem in which the great evangelist held her:

> Corrie is one of the great Christian heroines of the century. We met her in Switzerland, and her story made such an impression on Ruth that she recommended it to writers John and Elizabeth Sherrill. They jumped at it; and the book and film that followed brought home the horror of those days and the triumph of Christ's love in the midst of virulent hatred.[5]

However, according to Elizabeth Sherrill, the writing tandem became aware of Corrie's story through the meeting in Germany, not from a recommendation via Mrs. Graham.[6] Perhaps the evangelist meant to say that his wife recommended that the *book* be turned into the *movie* that Corrie had always wanted. In any event, the wheels were set in motion for a film as the book became a bestseller soon after its publication in November 1971.

It would be a huge undertaking for World Wide Pictures. World Wide Pictures, headed by Dick Ross, had been producing evangelistic films to accompany Graham crusades since the early 1950s. (Graham met Ross after the latter had produced a documentary film of the 1950 Portland crusade.) Many of these films ended with an altar call by Rev. Graham, and the ministry says that over the decade more than two million filmgoers have recorded a decision for Christ.[7]

During the sixties, the California-based World Wide Pictures, according to film critic Peter Chattaway, was "making a serious effort to produce films that would be shown in regular theatres and be taken just as seriously as regular Hollywood films." Some of these titles were *The Restless Ones* (1965), the last World Wide

Picture to be directed by Ross; *Two a Penny* (1967), starring British pop star Cliff Richard; and the humorous *For Pete's Sake* (1968).[8]

"Much of their artistic direction over the next two decades came from James F. Collier," Chattaway said, "who wrote the screenplay for *The Restless Ones* and directed many of the films that followed. In his films, he often looked for ways to push beyond the Billy Graham 'formula.'"[9]

Pam Moore, in her book *Life Lessons from the Hiding Place*, reproduced a 1972 letter from Corrie to a friend explaining her enthusiasm for the budding project. "Next week we go to Glendale to meet the people of World Wide Pictures," she wrote. "Billy Graham is very happy with the book and [thinks] that it can be worked out in a movie. It surely will reach many more people than we have ever been able to reach. I am so thankful. John and Elizabeth Sherrill's book is a good seller and has opened many doors and hearts for me. In April I will be 80 years old, and it seems that the Lord gives me more and more joyful work to do. I feel so privileged."[10]

One man who read the book and loved it was California newspaper executive Edgar Elfstrom. In June 1960 Elfstrom faced his own tragedy when his nineteen-year-old daughter, Brenda, was treated for a minor infection with an antibiotic called chloromycetin. Brenda, a student at the University of Southern California, developed aplastic anemia, a blood disease, and died. Elfstrom sued three physicians and a drug company, claiming that the antibiotic caused his daughter's death. In July, the drug company and the three doctors settled the case, and Elfstrom received checks totaling $35,000.[11]

One can only speculate, but perhaps Corrie's forgiveness of those who had hurt her so deeply had touched Elfstrom's heart.

Certainly, Casper's wise words to a young Corrie would have applied to his grief: "Do you know what hurts so very much? It's love. Love is the strongest force in the world, and when it is blocked that means pain. There are two things we can do when this happens. We can kill that love so that it stops hurting. But then of course part of us dies, too. Or we can ask God to open up another route for that love to travel." In any event, Elfstrom would find a way to bless many through another route for Corrie's book.

Around 1973 a new ministry, called Christians Inc., was incorporated in Orange, California, to receive gifts to Corrie's ministry and "help her with the flood of requests for help and appearances."[12] Corrie would use some of the funds that poured in to support other, lesser-known ministries and missionaries around the world.

In June 1973 she spoke at the Billy Graham crusade in Atlanta. By the time of the July 1974 International Congress on World Evangelization in Lausanne, Switzerland—the successor to the 1966 Berlin congress—Billy Graham was a glowing and vocal advocate of the life, ministry, and coming film about Corrie, when he introduced her with the following words:

> Seldom in one's lifetime does one have the privilege of meeting or working, and hearing, a person who is a legend in her own lifetime. Corrie ten Boom was the first official woman watchmaker in Holland. And during the Second World War, she and her family helped protect and save many Jews. Because of that, she and her family were condemned to the concentration and the death camps. Her father was killed, her sister, and the week that she was to die, she miraculously escaped. Since then, she has toured the world, preaching the Gospel of our Lord Jesus

Christ, winning many to Christ, by both her writings and her preaching, and now a motion picture has been made on her life, that we think is the finest religious motion picture ever made, and will be in contention, we believe, for an Academy Award this coming year. It'll be released early next year. It's called *The Hiding Place*. And many of you are going to want to see that in many languages. But Corrie ten Boom, there's a new book about her, and by her, called *A Tramp for God* [*sic*]. And I want to introduce her today as one of the great women that it's been my privilege to meet in secular or religious life, but I want to introduce her as what she fondly likes to be known as, a Tramp for God. Corrie ten Boom of Holland.[13]

The movie would come the following year.

However, on a human level, *The Hiding Place* film almost didn't happen. Months turned into years, and the film went nowhere. Walter Gastil, the first president of Christians Inc., told of a meeting of members of the board of World Wide Pictures to discuss the project. He said they had "just about made up their minds that it was [too] risky an undertaking, too uncertain, they were doubting whether they could raise the necessary funds to do the picture as it should be done. The amount of money required represented several times what they had ever risked on a single picture. This called for the filming of an extravaganza, a major production, and they were doubting their capacity to do something big."[14]

However, the board members hadn't counted on a fortuitous series of events that would change their fear into faith. Elfstrom had been negotiating the sale of *The Fullerton News Tribune* to Scripps Howard.[15] When the sale went through, the Elfstrom

Foundation had money available for charitable contributions. Gastil said the foundation, unbeknownst to World Wide Pictures, "elected to make a very substancial [*sic*] gift to Christians Incorporated with the express hope that these funds would be used to make the story of Corrie's life, during the days of World War II, into a movie, 'The Hiding Place,' if the Board . . . felt it wise."[16]

Elfstrom's foundation sent the money to Christians Inc. and to Corrie the day before she was scheduled to meet with the board of World Wide Pictures. The next day, Gastil said, Corrie told the BGEA's film arm that she had the money in hand and that Christians Inc. was "prepared to turn it over to World Wide Pictures if they were ready to go ahead with the movie." Gastil added, "When Corrie announced this fact, . . . it was like an electric shock, stimulating them to action."[17]

"They voted full speed ahead," he added, "regardless of cost with full faith and conviction that it was God's will. So it has proven to be. Although it cost a great deal of money, they never were lacking in funds to meet the bills."[18]

Back in January 1972, Corrie had told her ministry supporters, "God needs to do miracles in many ways: a scriptwriter, then finances, the right cast, and many other things."[19] The finances had finally come through. The other miracles would follow in due time.

The $1.7 million film was to be directed by Collier and would feature Julie Harris as Betsie, Arthur O'Connell as Casper, and Jeannette Clift, a Texas theater actress, as Corrie. Following her performance in *The Hiding Place*, Clift would receive a Golden Globe nomination for Most Promising Newcomer—Female. Harris was a veteran of many Hollywood movies, including *East of Eden* (1955), *Requiem for a Heavyweight* (1962), *The*

In the midst of an extremely busy and sometimes stressful schedule filming her story, Corrie shares a lighter moment with actress Jeannette Clift, who played her in The Hiding Place.

Haunting (1963), *You're a Big Boy Now* (1966), and *Reflections in a Golden Eye* (1967).[20] O'Connell had been nominated for an Oscar for Best Supporting Actor for both the films *Picnic* (1955) and *Anatomy of a Murder* (1959). His role as Casper ten Boom in *The Hiding Place* would be his last.[21]

Corrie was thrilled with the cast. Ellen de Kroon (later Stamps), her helper, said in a prayer letter to film supporters, "Jeannette Clift, a fine Christian lady, will play the part of Corrie. Betsie will be played by Julie Harris, who prayed years ago with Ethel Waters, to receive Christ. Arthur O'Connell, a well-know[n] actor, will be Father."[22]

Collier met with Corrie and Ellen in Amsterdam before the filming. De Kroon indicated that the film's evangelistic intent would include those connected with its making. "Pray for Jim Collier and all his assistants," she said. "Not all of them are Christians, but they are very nice and loving people. We have come to like them very much and trust the Lord to work in their hearts."[23]

The Hiding Place was filmed starting on March 10, 1974, on location. It began in bumps and starts. Corrie traveled to Holland early that February, before any of the cast or crew had arrived, but her eagerness didn't keep the production from experiencing about three weeks of delays. First came the ordinary logistical problems.

"They ran into great difficulty," Gastil said, "lining up the large number of people to play the 'bit parts'—street crowds [and] scenes in prisons and concentration camps." Vintage cars, military uniforms, and period clothing were also hard to come by.[24] The Beje had been modernized in the decades after the war and so was unsuitable for the picture.[25]

A bit of good news came, according to De Kroon, when "a beautiful street in Haarlem and just the right house" were found three blocks away. "It needs to be rebuilt in a short period of time," she said, "so prayer is requested for strength for the workers."[26]

Another, even more unique, challenge was finding Jewish people of the right age, as so many had been killed in Holland during the war.[27] De Kroon asked for prayer "that more Jewish people will be available. Some of the Jewish people who will appear in the film are the only ones who are still alive from their whole family. Pray that in moments of tension the love and peace of Jesus Christ will fill their hearts and those who don't know Jesus will see what the Lord can do through His children."[28]

Then the Arab oil embargo, which began the previous October, began to bite in Holland and in England. The British work week was cut to three days, which made it more difficult to film the inside scenes in a studio there. The delays and shortages added greatly to the movie's budget. The camp was re-created at an old mobilization center for British soldiers in southern England. Although her doctor recommended she not visit the set depicting the camp, Corrie ten Boom wanted to be there for the final days of shooting.[29]

"During all this," Gastil said, "Corrie's counsel was constantly needed. The Lord gave her super-human strength. In addition she ministered to actors, [the] technical crew, and workmen—with rewarding results."[30]

Yet it was not easy for Corrie, who experienced her trauma all over again. "So authentic were the German soldiers' uniforms and so real the film set," Moore recalled, "that when Corrie ten Boom first entered she exclaimed, 'For so many years I have talked about my experiences all over the world, yet I had dismissed those horrible nightmares from my mind. Today, it all suddenly comes back!'" She added, "It was difficult for me. The moment I entered the camp I felt it was all real again, maybe too real. It became too much for me. I couldn't hold my tears any longer, and maybe it was good that I cried."[31]

Finally, however, the translation of *The Hiding Place* onto film was done. In September 1975, Gastil noted that "a dream"— Corrie's dream that her book would be made into a movie—"after long pauses of uncertainty, finally has become a reality. We must thank the Lord for the miraculous way in which uncertainty became certainty, and His answer to the fervent prayers of Corrie, Ellen, and scores of other people who believed that the story of Corrie's life in prison would be a great instrumentality in leading thousands of people to find Jesus Christ as their Lord and Saviour." [32]

Unlike most other Graham films, this one would be stark, with no easy answers offered in the face of such evil. One reviewer said the film stuck closely to the book, no doubt helped in part by Corrie's presence. Location shooting in Holland, he said, gave *The Hiding Place* "a bleak, gritty sense of time and place. In huddled conversations in the camp, the film heightens the sense of abandonment by framing the actors' pale faces in a sea of darkness. Among stand-out scenes, a wordless pantomime exchange between Corrie and Betsie through a dirty infirmary window is one of the film's best moments." [33]

Those involved in the project, including Corrie, who with Stamps provided "untiring help," didn't try to dampen anyone's expectations. Gastil said that "all who have seen it have agreed [it] is the greatest religious picture that has ever been developed." [34]

What would regular theatergoers say? Corrie and the team would soon find out—although the film's unveiling, as with its production, did not go as smoothly as planned. World Wide Pictures contracted for showings at two thousand theaters across the country. Among the promotional efforts associated with the film, television interviews were booked for Corrie and some of the actors.

"We're confident to believe that the Lord will bless these activities," Gastil said, "and through this picture, many people will find their Lord and Saviour, and changed lives will result." [35]

The premiere was scheduled for September 29, 1975, in Beverly Hills. Gastil said that Billy Graham took personal charge of the events both before and after the showing, and that many celebrities had been invited from Hollywood, business, politics, and the churches. Also on hand would be his own friends and those of Corrie, those who had worked on the film, and members of the media. "This," Gastil said, "should bring favorable publicity and awareness of the picture all over the United States."[36]

But no one counted on another group that was planning to show up in Beverly Hills.

Hundreds of people were pouring into the theater. One of them was a cigarette-smoking teenager named Rita Mayell, the daughter of high-flying condominium developer Lionel Mayell. Just graduated from high school, she was a confused and questioning Christian who felt like a misfit when compared with other believers. Her parents took her to the film's premiere.

Before the showing, Rita was in the ladies room, in front of the mirror, when the door opened. In walked an octogenarian with piercing blue eyes behind wire-rimmed glasses. Rita turned, the two made eye contact, and the old woman pointed a bony finger at the teenager and said, "God so loves you!"

Suddenly, all the questions of this self-described "black sheep" didn't matter so much in her sudden realization of God's acceptance. "It was a pivotal point in my life when I needed to know God's love," Mayell said later. "It was a demonstration of God's love to me at a moment when I really needed to know that love."[37]

But Mayell didn't have the opportunity that evening to reflect on her life-changing encounter with Corrie ten Boom—or even watch the premiere. She entered the theater for the showing along with the buzzing crowds, eager to receive more encouragement from the Lord. Instead, Mayell suddenly couldn't see or breathe. A teargas bomb had been thrown into the crowd, causing the suddenly panicked theatergoers to make a rush for the exits.[38]

So the showing was postponed. Outside and separated from her parents, she remembers singing "His Eye Is on the Sparrow" with Ethel Waters and many others in a hastily arranged concert before the singer was taken to a local hospital in a police car.[39] Pam Moore says that hundreds of people were involved in the street meeting, including Corrie, Billy Graham, Pat Boone, George Beverly Shea, and Cliff Barrows.[40]

"We held an impromptu street meeting out in front," Billy Graham said in his autobiography, "while the police and fire departments attempted to find out what had happened. I spoke to the crowd and prayed."[41]

A neo-Nazi group was suspected of having thrown the canister, ruining the premiere. While the show did not go on that night, the reception afterward did. There Corrie was asked for her response:

> People asked me tonight, "What did you feel about this [teargas] bomb that was falling?" I was touched. I was sad. Do you know why? Not only because there was in some way disappointment for people who had hoped to see the film but because on that bomb was the Hakenkreuz, the [Nazi] swastika.
>
> What we have to do . . . is love these people who hate us—love them, pray for them. These people are wounded people who have hate in their hearts. They need forgiveness. They need the Lord. That is the answer we must give.[42]

As a result, Corrie, Gastil, and all who worked on and prayed for the project received even more publicity, as newspapers and television programs around the world described what had happened in Beverly Hills. Graham noted that *The Hiding Place* "premiered the following night without incident and has become the most widely seen motion picture we've ever produced."[43]

Although critic Steven D. Greydanus called *The Hiding Place* "one of the best films ever produced by a faith-based group,"[44] the film adaptation of Corrie's World War II story never won the Academy Award. But it did something of more lasting significance.

"The film," Corrie told *People* magazine's Lois Armstrong, "shows people how to come through with God in the difficult times ahead. The worst can happen, but the best remains."[45]

It's a lesson that Corrie ten Boom would continue to share—and learn—in her own life.

THREE

The Christian

Corrie ten Boom is known worldwide because of *The Hiding Place*, both the book and the movie. Yet this Dutch watchmaker lived her imperfect but bracing three-dimensional faith far beyond the walls of Ravensbrück.

CHAPTER 8

"KEEP LOOKING DOWN"

Brother Andrew, Corrie's old friend and ministry partner, had become chairman of her ministry's board. Andrew said he helped her start Christians Inc. after he turned down Corrie's request to join his own Open Doors ministry. Why? "She was too famous." After one of their board meetings, she strolled outside with Andrew, who later recalled some interesting advice from Corrie.

> We walked from the door to the street, through the gate, to where I'd parked my car. We stood there and shook hands and she said, "Andrew, keep looking down." I thought, "Corrie, you're old. We don't say that. We look up!" She saw my hesitation, and with a little more emphasis, she repeated, "Andrew, keep looking down." I thought, "Corrie, now I know you're getting old. You're out of touch." She saw my hesitation. She pressed my hand a little firmer, and with more emphasis she said, "Andrew, keep looking down! Look at the world from God's point of view. He doesn't see iron curtains. He doesn't see bamboo curtains. He sees one world and

He loves that world. He gave Jesus!" Then I understood how deeply . . . prophetic that was—keep looking down. It was a great lesson to me.[1]

As this remembrance shows, Corrie's character was one of persistent, in-your-face encouragement to trust God and try to see life from his point of view. She had always been a noted figure because of her experiences in the war and her willingness to go around the world to speak of Christ's victory no matter what. But her newfound celebrity would present a personal challenge for Corrie to "keep looking down."

Mrs. E. F. Elfstrom, wife of Edgar and a close friend of Corrie, said that the Dutch watchmaker was well aware of the allure of fame. "One time after a Christian meeting where she had received much adulation," Mrs. Elfstrom said, "Corrie surprised my husband and [me] by asking, 'How can I keep people from putting me on a pedestal?' And she meant it. Corrie never cared for the role of celebrity."[2]

Corrie, however, never shied away from her celebrity status. Instead, she tried to use it for the kingdom. Walter Gastil noted just before *The Hiding Place* was released on the silver screen that Corrie's popularity had already exploded, thanks to the book, which by this time had sold more than two million copies.

"While initially," Gastil said, "Corrie had to give most publishers a guarantee in advance to get her books published, today publishers everywhere are diligently publishing rights on terms most favorable to the ministry—books, tapes, records, and music. Today, these royalties represent a growing percentage of the resources for the ministry."[3]

Indeed. Corrie's 1974 book, *Tramp for the Lord*, sold an astounding seventy-seven thousand copies in the first two months.

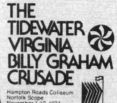

Despite Corrie's growing fame (here she was a featured guest at a Billy Graham crusade in Virginia), she tried never to let it go to her head, once asking a friend, "How can I keep people from putting me on a pedestal?"

With the film premiere looming, ministry leaders looked to gear up the book, tape, and film distribution of Corrie's messages and more strategically plan her speaking engagements to focus on large gatherings and national and international events.

"Corrie joyfully accepted invitations to speak to any group, no matter when, where or how small the group," Gastil noted, "but today, with thousands of invitations, she can choose the most promising opportunities. It becomes the responsibility of this Committee to harness increased resources to increased opportunity, providing much greater distribution of Corrie's messages."[4]

The Lausanne congress was far from her only opportunity that year. In November, Corrie spoke at the Billy Graham crusade in Tidewater, Virginia. Jeanette Clift, who would play her in the movie, was on hand as well. "As I watched [Corrie's] involvement in the filming of *The Hiding Place*," the actress said later, "I was amazed that she made so few demands. She didn't meddle with the details of what she believed to be God's movie. Instead, her prayers cut a path through obstacles and her blue eyes served as beacons to keep us on the track of truth."[5]

Among the new, larger speaking venues ministry leaders discussed for Corrie were conventions, such as Bill Gothard seminars; the Christian Booksellers Association; churches such as Melodyland in Anaheim; ministries with a broadcast component such as Robert Schuller's Crystal Cathedral in Garden Grove and Chuck Smith's Calvary Chapel in Costa Mesa; and other television opportunities, such as various Billy Graham crusades, *The 700 Club* on the Christian Broadcasting Network, and the charismatic evangelist Kathryn Kuhlman.[6]

The ministry also needed to standardize its policies, as money was pouring in from people awakened to her ministry through

The Hiding Place. Christians Inc. was receiving a growing number of financial requests from other ministries around the globe, and Corrie would often approve a request "wherever I see the need."[7] Corrie's interests were widespread. Several years later, Christians Inc. would allocate $8,800 to a Vietnamese missionary in Oregon, $5,000 to a Dutch missionary in Brazil, $6,500 to a missionary with CHIEF (Christian Hope Indian Eskimo Fellowship), $1,200 to an Indonesian missionary, $360 to three Ugandan evangelists, and $85,000 to the Association of Christian Prison Workers.[8]

The ministry noted that the requests had "greatly increased to the point where it was over-taxing Corrie's time, energy and health." Corrie also wanted to ensure that Christians Inc. didn't accumulate a surplus beyond its budgeted needs and the funds it allocated to specific projects.[9]

Standardizing the growing ministry's commitments involved a lot of nitty-gritty details, much like managing the watchmaking shop back at the Beje. For example, Christians Inc. agreed to negotiate its support for "The Hiding Place Library" at the Heidebeek, Holland, headquarters of a Youth With a Mission ministry called Dilaram Houses. The library would have on hand ten copies of each of Corrie's books and tapes in English, plus other languages as available. Other authors would be asked to contribute books as well. The project would require new shelving, painting and decoration, carpeting, and furnishings.[10]

In 1975, under a separate board, the Beje operated in Haarlem as a museum called "The Hiding Place," before closing in early 1977 due to logistical problems.[11] It would open again as the Corrie ten Boom House in 1987.[12] These kinds of issues were not the glamorous work of a Hollywood film premiere, but they were part of the tortuous process of making Corrie's enhanced ministry reach sustainable. A new book, *Prison Letters*, was also published.

Right after the movie was released, Corrie and Ellen began their monthlong fall speaking tour, and interest was immense. More than five thousand people turned out to hear Corrie in Albuquerque. While she was in New Mexico, Corrie spoke at a Santa Fe prison. Peggy Carter, her secretary, noted, "It is always such a joy for Corrie to be able to share God's love with those in prison." Then Corrie drew a crowd of fifteen thousand in Tulsa, where the film was also shown. A meeting in Jackson, Mississippi, filled the ten-thousand-seat coliseum, and all of Corrie's books were sold before the rally even started. Then it was on to New York, where Corrie was invited to participate in an installment of the TV game show *To Tell the Truth*.[13]

The next year, 1976, was also crammed with opportunities. Pam Rosewell (later, Moore) moved from Brother Andrew's ministry to become Corrie's full-time assistant after Ellen was married. In April Corrie received an honorary doctorate in Humane Letters from Gordon-Conwell Theological Seminary. Her books *In My Father's House*, about the first fifty years of her life, and *Corrie's Christmas Memories* were published. As well, a follow-up movie, *Corrie: Behind the Scenes with The Hiding Place*, was released.[14]

Corrie and Pam traveled together for seven months in Switzerland, Canada, and the United States, followed by three more in Holland. In November, Corrie said in an update to "Anne" from Florida how thankful she was to speak at the Pentagon, at "the nation's biggest top-security jail in Chicago," and elsewhere. "At all these places and many more I was able to bring the message God has put on my heart for the last 32 years. Often I have spoken about the riches we have in Jesus Christ (He is able to make *all* grace abound toward *you*) and the importance of being ambassadors for Christ."[15]

Pam, who had joined Corrie in the work only six months after the release of the film version of *The Hiding Place*, noted that Corrie was now widely recognized by Americans. "'Recognized' is too mild a word," Pam said. "Mobbed is perhaps more descriptive. For the extroverted Corrie this was no ordeal. The more people the merrier, as far as she was concerned."[16]

Corrie, who was now eighty-four, also shared with her ministry partners how she and Pam were getting along, and her hope to finally put down some roots. While she mostly lived out of her suitcases and traveled extensively in North America, Corrie's home base had always been in Holland. In 1967, an apartment in the Netherlands had been loaned to her for her use by a Dutch baroness.[17] After the success of her book, in 1974 Corrie eventually bought a three-story house with a garden in Haarlem,[18] to which she returned on Christmas and during summers[19] and would later sell.[20] She called it "Agape House."

"God is blessing Pam and me in our work together and we are a happy team," she wrote. "As to the future, our times are in God's hands. . . . I want to be based in California. I pray that the Lord will give us our own little house where we can work on making filmed messages, slide messages and doing more writing." As with most of her correspondence, she closed with the words that harkened back to the family tile in the Beje's dining room: "In Jesus, the Victor."[21]

Corrie was slowing down, preparing to travel less while continuing her ministry in some fashion. But whatever might happen, Jesus would remain victorious.

In January 1977, she and Pam received resident alien status in the United States. (Corrie's fidelity to the queen of the Netherlands was inviolable.) In February, Corrie located a small rental home in Placentia, California, naming it "Shalom House." In an

August letter to ministry supporters, she extolled her new home's garden with its orange trees and bougainvillea, healthy climate, and quiet surroundings, which, she added, were "conducive to accomplishing much."

"The work is going very well," she wrote. "Now that I do not have to give my time and strength to packing suitcases and travelling, I am able to work on books and films which the Lord has given me in order to reach many with the Gospel."

Indeed. That year the following books were published: *Each New Day*; *Prayers and Promises for Every Day*; *He Cares, He Comforts* (part of her Jesus Is Victor series); and *He Sets the Captives Free*. A film for prisoners, *One Way Door*, was also completed.

But Corrie's wanderlust was not easily cured, despite her comfortable new surroundings. That year, among her other commitments, she was a guest speaker at a Graham crusade in Sweden, spoke to prisoners in San Quentin, was named by CHIEF as an honorary member of the tribes, and, after being hospitalized in order to receive a pacemaker, spoke to a group in Oregon. Her ministry's dream of having Corrie appear on Pat Robertson's *700 Club* was also fulfilled.

Corrie described her contextualized message to the American Indians that July, when they gave her the Hopi name *Loma Si* (Beautiful Flower): "I . . . told them about the very greatest honor I have ever had in my life when I also received a name. That name was 'sinner saved by grace' and I was accepted into the tribe of Jesus Christ, became a child of God and could say, 'Father, my Father' to God. The Indians put a big feather headdress on my head and a shawl over my shoulders."[22]

In a letter that October, right after receiving the pacemaker, Corrie asked "Anne" to pray for her health and continuing ministry opportunities. She was conscious of God's grace in keeping her increasingly frail body alive. Corrie said, "My pulse was going slower until it was going approximately 20 times a minute at times. The choice was: go to Heaven or have this operation. The former would have been the most wonderful for me, but there is still so much work to do here, so I accepted the latter thankfully. I will be in Heaven for eternity and here I can help to build the Kingdom of God through books and films."

It seems likely that Corrie, now eighty-five, knew she was living on borrowed time. "It is an exceptional experience to receive your life back from the Lord," she said to Andrew. "I am more conscious than ever of being the Lord's property in the coming time which I, by His grace, may live." Over her signature Corrie closed with a slight variation on the familiar words, "In Jesus the Victor United."

Whatever might happen, Corrie ten Boom would keep looking down.

CHAPTER 9

A PRISONER ONCE AGAIN

As 1978 dawned, the honors were still accumulating for Corrie, even as her strength was slowly slipping away. On February 24, she would receive the Jane Addams award from Rockford College (now University). Addams had graduated from the Illinois school in 1881 (when it was named Rockford Female Seminary). Addams went on to a career in social activism that led to Hull House in Chicago and, in 1931, a Nobel Prize, making her the first American woman to be so honored.[1]

In a letter to Corrie, Rockford College described the award: "This award was established as a memorial to our most distinguished alumni and as the highest honor granted by the Rockford College is awarded to women of extraordinary accomplishment in an area of human, cultural and social life. The trustees were much moved by your life story as depicted in *The Hiding Place* book and thus wish to honor you for your selfless dedication to the value of human life during the second World War."[2]

Corrie, however, was unable to attend the ceremony, so she arranged for a prerecorded thirty-minute interview to be played at the school's convocation. After answering Rockford College's questions, she thought that "the interview went off beautifully and she was able to give a strong Christian testimony to this secular school."[3]

That summer, Corrie enthusiastically consented to a "This Is Your Life" ceremony in her honor hosted in Denver by World Wide Pictures and her publisher. Cliff Barrows of the Billy Graham Evangelistic Association was the master of ceremonies. Ruth Graham and Joni Eareckson were there, along with CHIEF's Tom Claus and friends from Holland, including her nephew, Peter van Woerden.[4]

At the end of the emotional evening, Corrie was presented with a large bouquet of yellow roses. Pam says her famous friend responded to the adulation characteristically: "She lifted the bouquet to the Lord and I knew she was saying to Him, 'Lord Jesus, this is yours.'"[5] The high altitude got to Corrie, however. Two days later, back in Placentia, she needed an oxygen tank.

Corrie had been no stranger to a variety of ailments and injuries over her eight and a half decades, in her own life and in the lives of loved ones. Pam kept careful count of them in the timeline she compiled of Corrie's family. Besides Betsie's "pernicious anemia," Tante Bep died of tuberculosis at age seventy; Corrie's mother had a slight stroke when Corrie was nineteen; Corrie had an appendectomy at twenty-two; and her mother had another stroke—a major one—when Corrie was twenty-six. This was just the beginning. Tante Jans died of diabetes at seventy-one, her mother died at sixty-three, Tante Anna died at sixty-four, Corrie had a terrible flu when the Gestapo arrested her at fifty-two, Casper died in prison at eighty-four, Betsie died in Ravensbrück at fifty-nine, Corrie suffered from edema in Ravensbrück, and Willem died at age sixty from tuberculosis of the spine (contracted in prison). Further, Corrie fell and injured her hip at age sixty-one and later endured an infection of the liver, and broken bones in an auto accident at the age of seventy-five. She was no stranger to physical suffering.[6]

At eighty-six, Corrie had survived all this, outliving everyone in her family who had come before. Her greatest challenge was just ahead, however. Yet even in this, Corrie would remain victorious. Pam tells the story that a couple of years before, Corrie had experienced a persistent dream that caused her to be quiet and reflective. "In my dream," she told her companion, "I am inside a room from which I cannot escape. I am permanently there and it is rather like a prison. While I am there my message is still going out to the people through films and books and television."[7]

Was it a premonition of what was to come because of the debilitating strokes suffered by her mother so many decades before? Or was the Lord she loved telling her, as he had told Peter by the sea,[8] in what manner she was to die before meeting him? Corrie had a mystical streak and expected to hear directly from God when necessary. In January 1978, after praying to see God's glory, she had received another message. One night at 11:30 while Pam was reading in bed before going to sleep, Corrie poked her head in the bedroom and said, "The Lord had been talking to me and I want to tell you about it."[9]

Corrie sat on Pam's bed and recounted her conversation with Jesus. "I asked the Lord if I must die soon. 'No, not yet,' was His reply."

Then Corrie asked if she would see something of him while she lived, as this would bring her much joy—joy that would redound to him in her film ministry. "Yes, you will see something of Me.'"

After asking about Pam, Corrie asked the Lord whether he was coming soon. "Yes, but you come first in heaven. Very shortly after that I will come again."

Whatever we are to make of this—whether Corrie actually heard verbally from the Son of God and what "very shortly" might mean for the Second Coming—clearly she expected to see *something* of him before she died. As she had experienced his goodness while a prisoner of the Nazi regime, she was soon to see him in an unexpected way while a prisoner in her own mortal flesh.

At 8:00 A.M. on August 23, 1978, Pam went into Corrie's still darkened room, bearing a tray with two cups of hot tea. They would never be enjoyed. Pam found to her horror that Tante Corrie, still in bed, was unable to speak or to move. At the same hospital where Corrie had received the pacemaker, Pam learned that Corrie had suffered a stroke, partially paralyzing her right side and ending her ability to express her thoughts verbally.[10] Early on, the odds of her survival were not favorable.

At 3:20 P.M., Corrie's friend and business associate Bill Butler of Christian Resource Management fired off a telegram to Brother Andrew in the Netherlands:

> corrie had a stroke early a.m. wednesday. in intensive care. verdict in 72 hours. will notify you. has not been made public. need statement from you for news release if necessary, re: her Life etc.[11]

Corrie *would* survive, but her trial was just beginning. Suddenly Pam's commitment to Corrie ten Boom was raised to a completely new level. Corrie had previously told Pam that she believed they would be together until Corrie went to heaven, but neither thought that it would be as a long-term caregiver. Following the stroke, Pam, along with Corrie's secretary Lotte Reimeringer, were on the front lines of the octogenarian's care. Hospitalization was followed by painstaking physical and speech therapy, and a slow recovery that included the ability to speak only a few words because of her severe aphasia. Speech therapy was discontinued. This was probably a painful blow to Corrie the communicator. Pam, however, said she was in "reasonably good health," good enough to be taken on local outings to the beach, a nearby canyon, and even Lion Country Safari—all of which "she enjoyed very much."[12]

On April 15, 1979, Corrie celebrated her eighty-sixth birthday. On May 30, she suffered a second stroke, which cost her the use of her right arm and leg. "I was standing by her this time," Pam said. "In a few seconds she had lost all the speech she had worked so hard to regain and was paralyzed on the right side. She was sufficiently conscious to make it clear that she did not want to go to hospital and in respect of her wishes the doctor allowed her to remain home." Corrie would rally again and eventually began to receive twenty-four-hours-a-day nursing care. Eating was painful and difficult because the muscles on the right side of her throat were paralyzed.[13]

"Her attitude in her very difficult circumstances is good," Pam reported to the board. "There are times of sadness and frustration at being unable to express even her needs or thoughts . . . but she looks to the Lord. We try to tell her of her ongoing vital ministry. In my own experience this does not seem to encourage her particularly. The only time we have response when trying to encourage her is by reading the Bible, praying, talking of the joy that lies before her."[14]

Not knowing how long Corrie might hold on, that summer her team began planning a memorial issue of *The Hiding Place* newsletter, asking Brother Andrew for a short contribution. He gave them three typewritten pages. He spoke about her greatness, which was manifested in her weakness. Corrie's weakness was on display for her daily caregivers. And so was her greatness.

"I remember how, in her healthy days, soon after she moved into her California home, she and I would take walks and discuss how, as she put it, we 'would be together until the wonderful end or, rather, the wonderful new beginning,'" Pam said. "I often wondered how that 'wonderful new beginning' would happen. I had always hoped, for her sake I thought, that it would be quick, but God in His great love allowed it to be slow by our human standards."[15]

While Corrie lingered in the valley of the shadow of death, she directed her friends to the Savior, whom she was no doubt seeing something of in her extremity. Pam and Lotte came to see that suffering and glory were closely related in the Bible, and in Corrie's frail life. Corrie still loved to hear God's Word and to pray. Though at times she seemed sad about what had happened, she accepted it rather than fought it as God's will for her. Hand gestures, facial expressions, and occasional words were her main forms of communication. Pam worked out a system of questions that would enable Corrie to indicate her wants and needs with the simple Dutch words *Ja!* and *Nee!*

"Always, even during great weakness and discomfort," Pam said, "Tante Corrie would point us to the Lord Jesus Christ. The peace which filled our home was a reality, a gift of the Lord."[16]

In her book *The Five Silent Years of Corrie ten Boom*, Pam marveled at Corrie's statement made when she had been forced into solitary confinement during the war: "My days of imprisonment will not be over until I have served my time." Corrie was serving a prison sentence of sorts as she sought the Lord's glory. "Had the Lord allowed her to come into this state of silence, helplessness, and utter dependence on Himself in order to show her more of His glory? We became more sensitive to watch for God's handiwork in this suffering, wondering how this seemingly endless situation was going to work out in conformity with His nature of goodness and love. . . . Could it be that this mysterious time in her life was not only for her own sake, but for the sake of the people immediately around her and of those to whom she was reaching out?"[17]

Then, in October 1980, the third and final stroke came. Corrie would not get up again. Yet her helpers continued to talk with her, read Scripture to her, and sing to her. Corrie would participate as best she could in her halting way. One day, Pam recounted, Lotte was sitting next to her bed. They were, Pam said, "talking about the fact that Jesus was Victor even in these very difficult circumstances." Lotte told Corrie that she didn't know a hymn with this theme, but perhaps the Lord would give them one. Right then Corrie closed her eyes in prayer. Several days later, "the Lord gave Lotte a hymn of several verses, in Dutch, which she translated into German and English, and which we sang to a seventeenth-century Dutch tune." Part of it went like this:

Jesus Christ alone is Victor
now and in eternity!
In His sovereignty He reigneth,
great in power and majesty![18]

Two and a half years of physical but not spiritual decline followed the third stroke. At about 10:30 P.M., with Lotte and Pam by her side, on April 15, 1983, Corrie's ninety-first birthday, the old Haarlem watchmaker's heart finally stopped ticking. Corrie went to her final hiding place and saw her glorious Lord face-to-face. Victory was finally hers. On her tombstone would be a simple inscription:

Corrie ten Boom
1892–1983
Jesus Is Victor[19]

According to Jewish tradition, dying on one's birthday is considered to be a particular blessing.[20]

CHAPTER 10

CORRIE'S CHARACTER

Corrie ten Boom's life can be described as having four distinct stages, each of which affected her character and ministry. Her quiet first fifty-two years can be described as *preparation*; her brutal ten months of Nazi imprisonment, as *persecution*; her thirty-three years of worldwide ministry, as *prominence*; and her nearly five years of physical decline after the first stroke, as *pilgrimage*.

For her first five-plus decades of life, Corrie loved her family, served many of her neighbors in active ministry, and grew into a mature, spiritually vital woman seeking Jesus the Victor above all. Corrie's brief but life-changing sojourn as a prisoner refined her understanding of God's love and care in a fallen world. Corrie's prominence gave her a platform to share the message of Jesus as Victor in a hurting world. Corrie's pilgrimage on a sickbed taught her and her caregivers that our value to God is constant and in no way depends on what we can do.

Pam Moore says Corrie lived a life of "complete surrender," with Betsie's statement about God's love being deeper than any pit as a touchstone for her life and message. Corrie spoke to God boldly, prayed frequently for the Lord to return, and was very careful to seek God's perspective. Once while traveling in

Moscow, Pam recalls, Corrie prayed, "Help me to see things more and more from Your point of view."[1]

Brother Andrew recalled that Corrie was never afraid to challenge him to do the same. Once he was visiting her in her stately house in Haarlem, filled with old clocks and family memories. There she had a beautiful garden, as well. As he was leaving, Andrew said, "Corrie, God is good to you!"

Corrie's face fell, and she seemed suddenly cross.

"Andrew," she replied, not using her friend's nickname, "God was also good when Betsie died."

Andrew got the point. "That was a very strong statement," he said. "The lesson I learned: That God is not only good when He does nice things to you. God is always good. Period! Because He is good. She applied it at once to Betsie, though we never even mentioned Betsie on that day. I don't know if she was always thinking about Betsie, but it must have occupied a major place in her memory."[2]

The Hiding Place provides several instances of Corrie the learner coming to see God's perspective in all circumstances. When Karel broke up with her for a young woman better situated financially, Corrie easily could have turned bitter. Instead, with her father's gentle encouragement, she made it a matter of prayer. "Lord," she prayed desperately, "I give to You the way I feel about Karel, my thoughts about our future—oh, You know! Everything! Give me Your way of seeing Karel instead. Help me to love him that way. That much."[3] And he did.

Another time, while in the Ravensbrück, Corrie and Betsie were moved to a new barracks—which they discovered was infested with fleas. They were also reading through the Bible, and Paul's command to "give thanks in all circumstances" (1 Thess. 5:18) arrested Betsie's attention. They were called to thank the Lord in *all* circumstances— even these. Betsie walked her younger sister through the litany. They thanked him for still being together, for having the Bible available to them, for the "suffocating crowds" (because the more would hear), and even for the fleas, though a reluctant Corrie could not fathom why.

In Barracks 28 were fourteen hundred female prisoners crammed together in a space designed for four hundred. They were pouring in from concentration camps in Poland, Austria, and elsewhere as the Nazis were losing their grip on Europe. The mix of languages and cultures, hunger, sickness, and fear led to much quarreling, even brawls, among the prisoners. So Betsie began to pray for the Lord Jesus to bring his peace to the place and take away the strife. Soon the backbiting gave way to cooperation. A multilingual worship service began, attended by Lutheran, Roman Catholic, Eastern Orthodox, and Dutch Reformed Christians. It was simple but powerful. Christ's light was shining in the darkness, and his prayer "that they may be one" (John 17:21) was being fulfilled, even at Ravensbrück.

Then one day they learned God's perspective on the fleas. The women who were able were forced to knit socks for the Germans. One day there had been confusion about the sizes of the socks, and the women asked the supervisor to come into Barracks 28 to resolve the issue. She refused, and so did the guards. Why?

"Because of the fleas!" Betsie said. "That's what she said, 'That place is crawling with fleas!'"[4] Now they knew why they had enjoyed such freedom to worship.

Yet having God's perspective often meant that Corrie had a clearer view of her own weaknesses and shortcomings—and like all members of Adam's helpless race, she had her share, sometimes telling her admirers, "This halo you are putting on me gives me a headache."[5]

Corrie had a temper. In *The Hiding Place* she told of the day when the women were required to level the muddy ground with their shovels. A female guard was mocking Betsie, who was too weak to carry much of the black muck in her shovel. Rather than be offended, Betsie replied, laughing also, "That's me, all right. But you'd better let me totter along with my little spoonful, or I'll have to stop altogether."

This reply enraged the guard, who grabbed her leather crop and whipped Betsie across the face and neck. This was too much for protective Corrie, who had already been feeling a "murderous anger." Without thinking, she picked up her shovel and went after the guard, who was facing in the other direction. But before she could get there, Betsie stopped her. As the guard turned and tossed the shovel back to the sisters, a welt began to swell on Betsie's neck, which was bleeding.

"Don't look at it, Corrie," Betsie said, covering the wound with her hand. "Look at Jesus only."[6]

Corrie would have to deal with a strong will and temper for the rest of her life. While they would at times serve the aging Dutch watchmaker well during her years of world travel and ministry, at times they got the best of her.

Elizabeth Sherrill says that Corrie had an amazingly quick mind that didn't always come through to others when using what she called her "Corrie ten Boom English." But with this mental suppleness came a downside—impatience. "I'd hear her snap at someone," Sherrill writes, "then see her wince with disappointment at herself. Since in the press of the moment there might be no time to set things right, Corrie had made an inviolable rule for herself. At the end of each day she asked forgiveness of anyone she could get in touch with . . . for a sharp word . . . a tactless remark . . . an unfair criticism . . . a hasty judgement."[7]

Elizabeth once asked her why she had to pray so often for patience. Shouldn't love, understanding, and self-control be permanent gifts for the Christian? "Oh, no!" Corrie replied. "He wants us to draw our supply fresh from him each day."[8]

Brother Andrew saw the impatient side of Corrie during his work with Christians Inc., especially when money was involved. Although her books sold millions of copies, Corrie never got rich from them, having to rent her last home (and not on the beach, because that was too expensive). When her ministry was facing a financial squeeze around the beginning of 1975, the former Dutch watchmaker who had organized Father's books decided she must end her promised support of a Bible institute project in Sweden. In February, Andrew wrote a note to Corrie and her team, urging her to at least pay the institution's debt taken on for the project— saying that she was "morally obliged to do that."[9]

In a September 1977 letter to Christian Resource Management about rising costs for a project translating and sending her books into Eastern Europe, Andrew urged patience. "I . . . notice that the cost is a lot more than originally anticipated," Andrew wrote, "and I hope that you will be able to soothe Corrie's feelings about this. Whenever you ask Corrie for more money than she intended to give, she gets very upset. . . . I don't want that to happen with this very important project."[10]

Whatever her failings and challenges, Corrie was secure enough to admit her mistakes and give them to Jesus the Victor. Elizabeth tells the story of Corrie needing to draw a "fresh supply" of God's power to forgive, even in the seemingly small things. Again it involved money.

We were staying with her in Holland, some time after *The Hiding Place* was published, when some old friends came for coffee. We knew some of her history with these people: once trusted co-workers, they'd cheated her out of lecture fees she counted on for her work with concentration camp victims.

Because they'd practiced the deception with smiles, she'd found it even harder to forgive them than the brutal Nazi guards at Ravensbrück. But she'd done it at last, she told us happily. "When we forgive others," she liked to say, "God forgives our sins and throws them into the deepest part of the ocean!"

It was a pleasant party with these old associates, seated in the glow of Corrie's coal-burning grate, hard feelings on her part and guilt on the friends' side nowhere in evidence. "Obviously," John said, as we cleared away the dishes after they left, "they've accepted your forgiveness."

Corrie shook her head. "They say there's nothing to forgive! They deny that they ever cheated me. But I can prove it!" She ran to her desk and rummaged in the bottom drawer. "I have it all down here in black and white!" She straightened up triumphantly, a sheaf of papers in her hand.

Gently, John took the papers from her. "Corrie!" he said. "Aren't you the one whose sins are at the bottom of the sea? And you keep the sins of your friends on record in black and white?"

I watched realization, then dismay, then shame play one by one across Corrie's stricken face. Eyes brimming with tears, she spoke—not to us, at that moment I'm sure she'd forgotten us—but to God. "Lord Jesus, who takes all my sins away, forgive me for preserving all these years the evidence against others!"

And for a few hallowed minutes the three of us fed pieces of paper into Corrie's coal fire.[11]

The ability to forgive was hard-won and consistent throughout her long life. On June 19, 1945, Corrie learned that a Dutch man named Jan Vogel, who had betrayed her to the Gestapo, had been sentenced to death. That day she wrote Vogel a letter offering him both her forgiveness and the hope of eternal life in Jesus the Victor.

"I have forgiven you everything," she wrote. "God will forgive you, too, if you ask Him. He loves you and sent His Son to earth to pay the price for your sins—to bear the punishment for you and me."[12]

Corrie's forgiveness of others—whether they had betrayed and imprisoned her or merely cheated her—was always mingled with the knowledge that she too was a sinner saved by grace. Such knowledge, if widely applied in our day, would be a tonic to an angry and divided world in which the goal of racial and political reconciliation is more theoretical than actual. Through bitter experience and sheer hard work, Corrie knew the truth of this command in the Sermon on the Mount: "Love your enemies and pray for those who persecute you" (Matt. 5:44). May the church of Jesus the Victor, in the spirit of Corrie ten Boom, "go, and do likewise."[13]

Sometimes the life lessons were not so easily graspable, yet Corrie held on to her belief that God knew what he was doing. In *The Hiding Place*, we see Corrie being prepared unknowingly in the little things of life for persecution and all that would come afterward. As Corrie noted later in her book *In My Father's House*, "A person doesn't spring into existence at the age of fifty; there are years of preparation, years of experience, which God uses in ways we may never know until we meet Him face to face."[14]

We see this preparation in her long talks with Father about trusting the Lord and giving to him our deepest hurts. We see it in her ministry to children and the disabled—those little esteemed in the world, who could not pay her back. We see it in her decision to love and protect Jewish people in defiance of the Nazi regime. We see it in her care for other prisoners and for Betsie. We see it in her decision to forgive those who had hurt her. We see it in her decision to show the love of Jesus the Victor to those whose lives had been torn apart by war, even those who had collaborated. We see it in her decision to persevere through every obstacle.

Elizabeth Sherrill, in the afterword to the 2006 edition of *The Hiding Place*, tells the story of one of Corrie's visits to her and John's home in Chappaqua, New York. Tibby and her thirteen-year-old daughter, Liz, were helping Tante Corrie unpack her things. From the bottom of the suitcase, Liz lifted a folded piece of cloth with loose threads, uneven stiches, and colors that didn't seem to match.

"What are you making?" Liz asked, bewildered.

"Oh, that's not mine," Corrie said. "That's the work of the greatest weaver of all."

Liz looked dubiously at the tangled mess.

"But Liz," Corrie told her, "you're looking at the wrong side!" She took the sorry thing from Liz's hand. "This is what our lives look like, from our limited viewpoint."

Then, with a flourish, Corrie shook open the cloth and turned it around to display a magnificent crown embroidered in red, purple, and gold. "But when we turn over the threads of our lives to God, this is what He sees!"[15]

From the time she was a little girl who didn't want to go to school to the time she was an old woman waiting to go to her eternal home, Corrie ten Boom had practiced and learned the spiritual discipline of offering the tattered threads of her life to Christ, who would weave them into a beautiful pattern seen best in hindsight. As this onetime obscure watchmaker did so, she died to her earthly agenda and embraced the heavenly agenda of the Victor, King Jesus. This was God's perspective on her life, and Corrie's, through her long decades of preparation, persecution, prominence, and pilgrimage.

FOUR

The Calling

Most of the books ever published are enjoyed by mere slivers of the general public before being quickly forgotten. A few of these books are fortunate enough to make it onto the bestseller lists. Fewer still sell millions of copies and see films and other spinoffs created in their honor. Only the rarest of volumes is both popular and profound, with enduring insights for future generations. *The Hiding Place* is such a book. Given Corrie ten Boom's legacy as described in this book and in her subsequent decades of life and ministry, what might God be calling *us* to do?

CHAPTER 11

EVANGELISM: DISPELLING THE DARKNESS

The Enlightenment began the Western world's slow decoupling from Christianity. In recent decades, the estrangement has begun to accelerate. In the United States, the share of those who claim Christian faith declined from 78.4 percent of the population in 2007 to around 70 percent in 2014—an amazing drop of about 1 percent each year. Over that same time, the number of religiously unaffiliated American adults—the so-called "nones"—has jumped from 16 percent of the population to 23 percent, or nearly one in four. Ed Stetzer of *Christianity Today* calls this era "America's Age of Skepticism."[1] It appears that the West's inward turn and embrace of values that eye religious faith with skepticism since World War II have only deepened.

Ironically, the secularizing trend is far more advanced in Corrie ten Boom's native Holland. In a land where surprising numbers of Dutch people hid Jews from the Nazis out of Christian conviction—one estimate says that many of the estimated fifty thousand to sixty thousand people who were active in the Dutch underground were motivated by their Christian faith[2]—today the church in the Netherlands is all but dead. One recent survey found that fewer than one in three Hollanders say they have religious faith of any kind, and almost one in four say they are atheists. Meanwhile, the share of people describing themselves simply as spiritual fell from 40 percent in 2006 to 31 percent in 2016.[3]

In the face of these alarming numbers, fewer and fewer American Christians believe that sharing their faith with non-Christians is a personal responsibility. According to the Barna Group, back in 1993, nearly nine in every ten Christians who *had* shared their beliefs with someone else agreed that this is a responsibility of every Christian. But in 2018, only about two in three believed this—a 25 percent plunge in just twenty-five years.[4] And this decline occurred among those who actually *did* speak up!

Barna points out that these Christians are more likely to see social barriers to sharing their faith. They are more likely to agree that evangelism is effective only when there is a relationship with the other person (47 percent now vs. 37 percent in 1993). They say they would avoid a spiritual conversation if they knew their non-Christian friend would reject them (44 percent vs. 33 percent).[5]

So our secularizing culture is making people less open to and interested in the Christian gospel. At the same time, it is making Christians less willing to share it with friends and neighbors. Given both these trends, can the experience of the Netherlands be far behind in a country whose motto is "In God We Trust"?

"The overarching cultural trends of secularism, relativism, pluralism and the digital age are contributing to a society that is less interested in religion and that has marginalized the place of spirituality in everyday life," says Roxanne Stone, Barna's editor in chief. "As a result, Christians in America today have to live in the tension between Jesus' commands to tell others the good news and growing cultural taboos against proselytizing—a core part of Christianity from its origins and, many practicing Christians believe, [an action that is] essential for the salvation of their listeners."[6]

Given all this, *The Hiding Place* and the life of Corrie ten Boom have much to say to us. But we must recognize that Corrie lived in a much different world than we do, so her words and actions won't have unlimited applicability to ours. She was born before two world wars that would wreak havoc on a continent, destroying many of its institutions and assumptions about life. While the Dutch church was already undergoing liberalizing trends, it was easier to be a vocal and committed Christian. Key social communities such as family and church were stronger. Divorce was a relative rarity. The clergy were held in higher regard and were not steeped in scandal. The Bible was generally trusted. Faith in Christ, while always a hurdle for sinful people, was still *thinkable*. At the least, it was respectable.

Yet we need to remember that the Christian faith that Corrie knew and practiced was far from automatic. She recounts in *The Hiding Place* how she asked a local pastor to take an endangered Jewish mother and her baby into his home. The threat of Nazi punishment if he were discovered was very real. "No," he replied. "Definitely not. We could lose our lives for that Jewish child!" At that moment, Father walked in and said, "You say we could lose our lives for this child. I would consider that the greatest honor that could come to our family."[7]

Such faith regardless of the consequences was also on display when Corrie was imprisoned by the Nazi regime. In her conversations with Lieutenant Rahms in Scheveningen Prison, Corrie was bold about her faith and his need to trust in Jesus. The morning after telling this officer that the Bible reveals a God who cares for the weak and mentally challenged, Corrie stood before him again. It was the Gestapo officer who would be doing the confessing that day.

"I could not sleep last night," Rahms said to Corrie, "thinking about that Book where you have read such different ideas. What else does it say in there?"

"It says," Corrie answered slowly, "that a Light has come into this world, so that we need no longer walk in the dark. Is there darkness in your life, Lieutenant?"

After a long silence, the man replied, "There is great darkness. I cannot bear the work I do here." Then Rahms told the prisoner about his family in Bremen and his worries about them because of the war.

"There is One who always has them in His sight, Lieutenant Rahms," Corrie replied with the courage supplied by Jesus the Victor. "Jesus is the Light the Bible shows to me, the Light that can shine even in such darkness as yours."[8]

Corrie's courage to speak of the Truth to a Nazi officer who held her life in his hands would not fail her in the coming decades. After the war, Brother Andrew recounts, Corrie was speaking at a cathedral in Karl-Marx-Stadt (now Chemnitz) in communist East Germany.

They saw the church was going to be too crowded and there would be a big overflow. Corrie wanted to reach them. Quickly she went to the city council—they were probably in session at that time. She marched in there and she said, "I want a loud speaker system." Of course, in communism you didn't do that. Religion was okay, but only within the four walls. They objected and said, "Miss ten Boom, we cannot do that." She looked at them and said, "I need and I want a loud speaker system so that all the people in the square can hear me, because Jesus is the Victor! You know that, don't you!" They looked at her in total astonishment and then said, "Ja, Ja." Within a few minutes she had permission and they hurriedly put up big loud speakers and the whole square could hear Corrie preach that day.[9]

One might even say that what Corrie displayed when speaking about Jesus the *Overwinnaar* wasn't courage. It was *faith*—confidence that the Jesus who had been with her when she was imprisoned would be no less with her when she was free. Her confidence, which was forged in the long decades of peaceful but productive preparation, had been tested and found genuine in the brief but burning fires of persecution.

This woman of faith was ready to share Jesus the Victor with any who asked. Pam tells of the time in 1971 when a popular nonreligious television program in the Netherlands invited Corrie to come on as a guest. Few people in her home country had shown an interest in her story, so Corrie was excited to accept the invitation to talk about her travels and to give a short Easter message.

> Because it was not a Christian television program, I reached many people who were not expecting to hear such a message—perhaps six million people, I was told [nearly half of the population of Holland at the time]. The results were tremendous. Letters, phone calls and visits made the next weeks full of important work for Ellen and me. Many people who needed spiritual help came for counseling. Doors and hearts opened in churches and groups. Many found the Lord Jesus. People who had seen me on the TV invited me to come to various cities. And many people with whom I have had contact during various periods of my 79 years now got in touch with me again, including the people for whose salvation I had prayed decades before.[10]

She would share her confidence in Jesus the Victor during her decades of prominence, and she would be no less confident in her quiet years of pilgrimage. Pam provides a glimpse of Tante Corrie's evangelism when they moved into Shalom House. "During the first week at the house," Pam writes in *The Five Silent Years of Corrie ten Boom*, "Tante Corrie said, 'Let's go and meet the neighbors and take them one of my books.' I was a bit startled at this confident approach until I realized that there was absolutely no ego involved."[11]

Corrie ten Boom was a faithful evangelist her whole life. She told others about Jesus the Victor during her long years of preparation—girls who participated in Christian ministries started by her and Betsie and the mentally disabled who had nothing that the world valued. During Corrie's months of persecution, *The Hiding Place* describes her bold witness about her Lord and his Word to a searching Lieutenant Rahms. Her brave harboring of God's chosen people in defiance of the Nazis was ultimately a decision to cast her lot with her crucified, risen, and victorious Savior. It was also a form of witness that ultimately gave her a platform in the coming decades to tell others about the Light who had come into her world—the Light that she sought during her quiet years of pilgrimage.

Nothing stopped Corrie from being a witness for her Lord— not obscurity or celebrity, peace or persecution, sickness or health, love or hate, friend or foe, indifference or misunderstanding, wealth or poverty. Corrie knew her Lord and was determined to share him with others, no matter the circumstances. May we know and do the same.

Once when traveling in Communist East Germany after the war, her boldness came through when she was speaking from the pulpit of a cathedral. After she finished her speech, one of the theologians stood up and asked her whether she thought that women should be silent in church, as the apostle Paul had taught. She replied with conviction, "Alleluia, *Nein!*"[12]

Whatever you think of women's roles in the church, it's clear that Corrie possessed something many of us will never have—a faith tested and proved genuine by the hottest fires known to mankind. And it showed. Her words about Jesus the Victor thus were confirmed by her life and burned into countless hearts, even those of people who thought they had no need of a Savior.

These are challenging times for those who call themselves Christians, even in the relatively free and prosperous West. While our opposition is not as clear and brutal as the Nazi and Communist regimes that confronted earlier generations, it is no less real. And like the Christians from different faith backgrounds at Ravensbrück who came together in Jesus the Victor, in this hour of danger perhaps we will need to lay aside some of our nonessential doctrinal distinctives in the larger cause of Christian unity. Secular culture, like the serpent in the Garden, is winding itself around the hearts and minds of more and more people, ready to crush the spiritual receptiveness of any who wonder if Jesus might have anything meaningful to say in a divided and anxious world. Let's show them that he does.

Rod Dreher, author of *The Benedict Option*, is calling for a determined renewal of faith in the face of resurgent skepticism and crumbling religious institutions. "All Christians in the West—not just Catholics—must prepare ourselves for the decline, and even the fall, of our institutions," Dreher writes. "It's happening now. It's going to get worse."[13] But he says there is hope, and indeed there is. Corrie ten Boom shows us that Jesus is Victor over all human systems, worldviews, and heartaches. He is the source of Truth and grace (John 14:6), the answer to human longing.

He is also the answer to our age's plaintive cry for social justice. As with the struggle for civil rights, Christians don't always do what their Lord requires of them. Missionaries, too, have sometimes been blamed for not living up to the selfless standard of Jesus, who opened the eyes of the blind and set the captives free (Lk. 4:18). As the anticolonial activist Jomo Kenyatta said wryly, "When the missionaries arrived, the Africans had the land and the missionaries had the Bible. They taught us how to pray with our eyes closed. When we opened them, they had the land and we had the Bible."[14]

Southern Baptist church planter Doug Ponder says that in our postmodern age many people are no longer asking whether Christianity is *true*. Now they want to know if it is *good*. In response he cites researcher Robert Woodberry, who studied the fruit of Protestant missionaries before concluding that the answer, assuredly, is *yes*. "Areas where Protestant missionaries had a significant presence in the past," Woodberry says, "are, on average, more economically developed today, with comparatively better health, lower infant mortality, lower corruption, greater literacy, higher educational attainment (especially for women), and more robust membership in nongovernmental associations."[15] That's true social justice.

In our post-truth age, Christians seeking to follow Corrie's example as described in *The Hiding Place* and by the rest of her literary output and life may not have her testimony, but we have her Savior, who promises to redeem our dark times for his glory. We can trust him to help us spread his Good News even as he helped her do the same, no matter what. As Corrie said, "The worst can happen, but the best remains."

—

CHAPTER 12

ANTI-SEMITISM: DEFENDING HUMAN DIGNITY

Anti-Semitism has been called the oldest hatred. It is certainly among the most enduring. Haman tried to wipe out the captive Jews in the Persian Empire. In Alexandria, Manetho, a third-century-BC Egyptian priest, wrote viciously against the city's large Jewish diaspora. From the Middle Ages forward, the Roman church launched a series of bloody pogroms and inquisitions against the Jews.

In his later years, even the great Reformer Martin Luther said in *On the Jews and Their Lies*, "Set fire to their synagogues or schools." Jewish homes should "be razed and destroyed." Jewish "prayer books and Talmudic writings, in which such idolatry, lies, cursing, and blasphemy are taught, [should] be taken from them."[1]

In the supposedly more enlightened twentieth century, of course, Adolf Hitler inspired the Third Reich and many across Europe to slaughter six million Jews. Corrie ten Boom and the members of her family were among the relative few to stand against this monstrous evil.

Despite repeated, heartfelt cries of "never again," anti-Semitism continues to cast its shadow over our world. According to the Federal Bureau of Investigation, religiously motivated hate crimes show no signs of ending anytime soon. While Jews constitute a mere 2 percent of the US population, the FBI says they absorb more than 50 percent of all religiously motivated hate crimes.[2] The grisly October 2018 massacre at Pittsburgh's Tree of Life synagogue is a stark reminder that "the oldest hatred" refuses to be relegated to the history books.

In recent years, about two-thirds of such acts have targeted Jews or their houses of worship (numbers far higher than attacks against Muslims). A 2013 study for the Anti-Defamation League found that 14 percent of American adults agreed with the statement that "Jews have too much power" in the nation. Fifteen percent said Jews are "more willing to use shady practices." Thirty percent said American Jews are "more loyal to Israel" than to the United States.[3]

Anti-Semitism is still alive in Europe, fueled in part by increasing Muslim immigration. In the United Kingdom, one watchdog group reported a 34 percent rise in violent assaults against Jewish people in 2017.[4]

Combined with this animosity toward Jews is a troubling ignorance about the Holocaust itself. According to researchers at the United States Holocaust Memorial Museum, only half of American adults surveyed knew that six million Jews had died during the Holocaust. A third believed that the death toll was no more than two million. Further, 45 percent couldn't name a single concentration camp or ghetto (there were forty thousand such places during the war); 41 percent could not identify Auschwitz.[5]

Given all this, Corrie ten Boom's countercultural commitment to God's chosen people remains a bracing challenge to our times, and our hearts. John Wilson, formerly of *Books & Culture* and *Christianity Today*, says that *The Hiding Place* should be set alongside Anne Frank's *Diary* as a needed impetus to self-examination. Not everyone agrees. Wilson says that during the early seventies, while a student at California State University, Los Angeles, he was talking with a fellow graduate student about the difficulties in writing about Holocaust literature.

The man happened to be Jewish, and he described *The Hiding Place* in very negative terms. "In his view," Wilson recounted, "it provided a way for Christians to feel good about themselves, by identifying with Corrie ten Boom, when in fact the vast majority of Christians didn't respond as she and her family did: the very notion of an inspirational book connected with the Holocaust nauseated him." Wilson, however, thinks the book can serve a larger purpose. "I agreed that some people would no doubt read the book superficially," Wilson said, "but I thought it was an important story to set alongside (not to negate or paper over) many others—and that if read rightly, it was a challenge to readers . . . to examine their own hearts. Its application wasn't at all limited to the Nazi era."[6]

So how does the book's portrayal of a pietistic Christian woman's decision to protect and suffer for the Jewish people apply today, especially to Christians? Are we as interested in the Jews as were Corrie's readers, many of whom were caught up in end-times fervor?

First, of course, we must agree with Isaac da Costa, the ten Boom family, and the witness of the Bible itself—that God still loves the Jewish people and isn't done with them yet. We must also agree that this truth bestows a significant responsibility on followers of the Jewish Messiah to love them as *he* does. As Corrie said to a representative of the Jerusalem Prayer Team (one of the many ministries she supported), "You can't love God without loving the Jewish people."[7] Our love for the Jews must, as Corrie's did, go beyond sentimental or theologically correct words. It must involve tangible, and perhaps costly, actions.

It is simple enough to get started. First, do we and our churches know and regularly interact with our Jewish neighbors? Do we know what's important to them? Do we understand their history (which includes the nauseating history of Christian persecution), and not just via our understanding of the Hebrew Scriptures? Are we familiar with their feasts and holy days? Do we go to Jewish weddings and funerals? Do we genuinely care for Jewish people, regardless of their response to Jesus?

Second, it means we must stand up to anti-Semitism, wherever and whenever it appears. When someone makes an off-color or bigoted remark about Jews, do we say something? If a synagogue is attacked, do we stand with the rabbi and congregation? Are we careful in our services about how we refer to Jews, or do we carelessly blame them for the death of Christ? Do we assert that the Old Covenant has been completely done away with and is no longer of any use to Christians? Do we weigh how our words will sound in Jewish ears? And if, God forbid, something like the Nazi horror were ever to reappear, would we be willing to lay down our lives as the highest honor our Lord could bestow upon us?

I once wrote an article advocating the continued practice of evangelism of Jewish people by Christians, saying that Paul's gospel formulation of "to the Jew first" has not been rescinded.[8] The response was unexpected. Yehiel Poupko, a prominent rabbi in Chicago, asserted that such words must be seen in historical context, and that they had been used over the centuries to justify the idea that Jews, rather than being specially significant in God's eyes, "are lower in God's economy than any other people."[9]

Poupko is far from the only Jewish person who feels this way. Hebrew University of Jerusalem scholar Yaakov Ariel, for example, looked at several Christian Holocaust memoirs and said that Dutch Protestants, including Corrie ten Boom and her family, believed that the Jewish people had brought the Holocaust upon themselves by their rejection of Jesus as their Jewish Messiah. These Christians, he asserted, minimized the moral horror by believing that the catastrophe was caused not by anti-Semitism but by man's alienation from God.[10]

Yet there is no evidence in *The Hiding Place* or in Corrie ten Boom's life, nor in the lives of her family members, for this assessment. On the contrary, as Regent University scholar K. Alan Snyder said in a rejoinder to Ariel: The family's respect for the Jews and recognition of anti-Semitism were seen clearly in her brother Willem's career, which documented and responded to Europe's growing anti-Semitism. Before the war Willem ran a nursing home open to elderly people of all religions; in the 1930s it became a refuge for Jews escaping from Germany.[11]

Willem's thesis was titled "The Birth of Modern Racial Anti-Semitism in France and Germany." In it, Corrie's brother wrote, "I expect that in a few years' time, there will be worse pogroms than ever before. Countless Jews from the east will come across the border to seek refuge in our country. We must prepare for that situation."[12] Willem and all the ten Booms stood up to anti-Semitism, and so must we.

Third, it means we must be willing to humbly accept our connection with those who perpetrated historical anti-Semitism in the name of Christ. We must accept the painful and embarrassing historical fact that much Jewish suffering has come at the hands of Christians. We must accept the possibility that we would have done no better. As I have written elsewhere:

Rabbi Yehiel Poupko . . . reminds me that modern Christians are heirs of those so-called Christians who persecuted Jews down through the centuries. He has told me he knows *I* would never harm a hair on his head, and of course he is right. And yet I have an uncomfortable connection, a responsibility, for my anti-Semitic forebears. Would I do any better than they? I pray that I would. But do I *know* in my heart of hearts that if I lived during the first Crusade, I would not have murdered defenseless Jews who were "killed like oxen and dragged through the market places and streets like sheep to the slaughter"? No, I do not. Do I know beyond a shadow of a doubt that I would have opposed public lynchings of blacks who "didn't know their place" during the detestable era of Jim Crow? Do I?[13]

This brings us to a fourth application. Corrie ten Boom never intended to be a hero. She wasn't planning to do what she could to protect Jews from extermination. Circumstances forced her into action and revealed what was in her heart—circumstances, along with her relationships with Jews and her settled convictions about their worth and her duties to those who were "the apple of God's eye."

How about our convictions? Though, like Corrie, we don't know the future, we do know the Victorious One who holds the future in his hands. Are we prepared, when he calls, to stand up, as Corrie did, to defend people made in God's image when the state or the society around us threatens them? They might be Jews, but they might not be.

Are we prepared to defend the sanctity of human life? America has seen the legal extinction of roughly sixty million unborn human lives since the Supreme Court handed down its infamous *Roe v. Wade* decision in 1973, just two years after *The Hiding Place* was published. We have no record of what Corrie ten Boom thought about this, though her concern for children was evident in the book and throughout her life. Are we willing, as she was, to stand up to the powers that be at great personal risk? Is our conviction to honor Jesus in this matter sturdy enough to endure mockery and even persecution to protect the "little ones" he loves?

Are we prepared to protect others who are just as precious to God? Will we defend those who, because of their ethnicity, sex, or religious beliefs, face the loss of their dignity, rights, or livelihoods? Will we speak up for those unjustly imprisoned and trafficked so that their bodies can be consumed and discarded? Will we oppose the totalitarianism, racism, and nativism still poisoning God's world? Will we support the ethical and just treatment even of illegal immigrants? Are we prepared to love the poor and despised as Corrie did? Will we, unlike too many of our forebears, defend the civil rights of all?

The Hiding Place reminds us that we, like Corrie, are called to identify with our neighbors, whoever they are. Elizabeth Sherrill writes about the day one of the Jews whom Corrie had befriended and saved at the Beje, Meyer Mossell (Eusie in *The Hiding Place*), invited them to his home for tea. At one point Mossell opened the drawer of an antique sideboard and retrieved a scrap of yellow cloth that had been fashioned many years before into the shape of a star. "All these years I wondered why I saved this thing," Eusie said in Elizabeth's recounting. "Now I know it was to give it to you, Corrie."[14]

—

CHAPTER 13

REFUGEES: WALKING WITH THE SOJOURNERS

Corrie ten Boom knew what it was like to have a secure and loving home. She also knew what it was like to be snatched from that home as a prisoner under the bleakest, most dangerous circumstances imaginable. When Corrie returned home from Ravensbrück while Holland was still under occupation, she finally knew the bitter feeling of realizing that the Beje was not her real home.

One of the underground leaders warned her to expect changes at the Beje. A series of homeless families had lived there. The watch business had stopped. The family cat was missing, and the rooms were empty. Corrie restarted the business and took in some of the city's "feeble-minded," knowing they were at risk from the Nazis.[1]

Yet life at the Beje was unalterably different. Like Frodo returning from his quest to destroy the Ring, only to find his beloved Shire spoiled, Corrie knew that the Beje would never again be the place of belonging that she had remembered.

The world had already moved on. In *The Hiding Place* she recalls:

And still my restlessness continued. I was home, I was working and busy—or was I? Often I would come to with a start at my workbench to realize that I had sat for an hour staring into space. . . . I spent less and less time in the shop; whatever or whoever I was looking for was not there.

Nor upstairs. I loved the gentle people in my care, but the house itself had ceased to be home. For Betsie's sake I bought plants for every windowsill, but I forgot to water them and they died.[2]

Corrie's years of preparation and persecution taught her that she was a sojourner in this world, and that her true home was in heaven. Perhaps that realization is what caused her to move on after the war in her years of prominence to become what she called a "tramp for the Lord." Knowing she had no permanent home here, she was able to absorb discomfort and hardship while she sought to bring along others to the only hiding place that would last. She would keep going, no matter what.

Once, during a stopover at her Haarlem home, she telephoned Andrew, asking him to come over after church and pray with her. "I have some cracked ribs," she explained, "and I'm in great pain and cannot travel any more."[3]

In 1967, she ministered with Andrew in Vietnam, which was in the midst of war. Andrew said that the roaring of jets, the bombing, and the strafing brought back a lot of unpleasant memories to Corrie.

"Everything scared her," he said, "although she did not share that with the people to whom she was ministering. Bravely she would go out to the soldiers and to the tribes, and—with a great big smile—speak about the love of Jesus. But every day it was a battle for her to get up. And, very often in the mornings, I would have to lay hands on her and pray for strength, courage, love, faith, and endurance. She was so very aware of needing the power of God. She well knew that God ministers through people, even the weakest."[4]

Andrew noted, "Somehow she was conscious of the fact that being alone, being a woman, she was very vulnerable, in a world where she somehow had to make it on her own, where everything had been taken away from her, and where she had gone through a time of intense suffering in a concentration camp."[5]

Corrie's experiences in *The Hiding Place* and afterward as a sojourner have much to say to our time. According to the UNHCR, the United Nations agency for refugees, there are about 68.5 million forcibly displaced people around the world, representing an increase of 2.9 million in just one year.[6] The total is roughly equal to the population of France, Thailand, or the United Kingdom.

Of that 68.5 million, 25.4 million are refugees—each is "someone who has been forced to flee his or her country because of persecution, war or violence. A refugee has a well-founded fear of persecution for reasons of race, religion, nationality, political opinion or membership in a particular social group. Most likely, they cannot return home or are afraid to do so. War and ethnic, tribal and religious violence are leading causes of refugees fleeing their countries."[7] Two-thirds of these refugees originate from just five nations: Syria, Afghanistan, South Sudan, Myanmar, and Somalia.[8]

There are also, among the 68.5 million, about 40 million internally displaced people (IDP). An IDP is "someone who has been forced to flee [his or her] home but never cross an international border. These individuals seek safety anywhere they can find it—in nearby towns, schools, settlements, internal camps, even forests and fields. . . . Unlike refugees, IDPs are not protected by international law or eligible to receive many types of aid because they are legally under the protection of their own government."[9]

Finally, there are 3.1 million people seeking asylum by fleeing their own countries—including 1.7 million new claims in 2017. They must demonstrate that their application is based on a well-founded fear of persecution in their home countries.[10]

All told, the UNHCR reports that one person in every 110 worldwide is either an asylum-seeker, an internally displaced person, or a refugee. On average, every two seconds, somewhere in the world another person becomes displaced.[11]

In the face of this escalating global crisis, the United States appears to be stepping back from its role as the global leader in accepting refugees. According to the US Department of State, in fiscal year 2018, the nation accepted only 22,491 refugees, fewer than half the number of refugees admitted (53,716) in the previous fiscal year—and just over a quarter of those received in fiscal year 2016 (84,994). In department records dating back to 1975—the same year *The Hiding Place* film was released—only 1977 saw fewer people resettled as refugees to the United States.[12] Apparently fewer Americans and their leaders see the country as a hiding place for the displaced.

One of the guiding philosophies of the American experiment, of course, was captured on the Statue of Liberty, within easy sight of New York's Ellis Island, where so many immigrants arrived to build their lives and contribute to the young nation's greatness. On this colossus were inscribed the immortal words of poet Emma Lazarus, fairly bursting with America's growing confidence and hope:

Give me your tired, your poor,
Your huddled masses yearning to breathe free,
The wretched refuse of your teeming shore.
Send these, the homeless, tempest-tost to me,
I lift my lamp beside the golden door!

Today, much like the years leading up to Corrie's classic book, much of that national confidence seems to be gone. Some of it, no doubt, has been torn away by military quagmires in places as far afield as Vietnam and Afghanistan. Still more has been eroded by the terrorist attacks on September 11, 2001, as well as by subsequent bloody incidents perpetrated by radicalized Muslims on American soil. Though the Soviet Union is no more, there are more than enough dangers to spare. Prudence in this new era of global threats dictates that even our most benign impulses be gone over thoroughly in the service of national security and protecting the lives of all who are lawfully on American shores.

But it is certain that Corrie ten Boom had a heart for the powerless. She would want the vulnerable protected, just as she sought to protect the vulnerable—whether they were Jews, Christians, the mentally challenged, the elderly, or others.

After the war, Corrie sought to fulfill Betsie's dream of providing a big house in Holland where those damaged by life in the concentration camps could come and heal. The house would have large, sunny windows and opportunities for the residents to plant flowers, which Betsie thought would be especially healing to their souls. In 1945 Corrie would open such a house in Bloemendaal, called *Schapenduinen* (Sheep Dunes), as a Christian rehabilitation center for war victims.[13]

Another of Betsie's dreams was to repurpose a concentration camp in Germany so that those whose minds had been warped by

Nazi ideology could learn another way to live. In 1949 Corrie began ministering to refugee camps in Germany. That year she also rented and opened a former concentration camp in Darmstadt to serve more refugees. There she was able to share the Good News of Jesus with a legless and bitter German lawyer who could not claim "the victory of Jesus over fear and resentment" until Corrie honestly shared her own struggles.[14] The Evangelical Sisterhood of Mary served the refugees in Darmstadt until the camp closed in 1960.[15]

As a follower of the Book, Corrie would no doubt seek to follow God's heart for sojourners, who were specially protected in God's economy (Lev. 19:4). She would notice that Jesus, Joseph, and Mary were displaced for a time when fleeing the fury of Herod. She would remember her own family's bitter experience of being uprooted and driven into death camps, and her willingness to risk her own safety for others.

If she knew of it, she would no doubt have been horrified to learn of the Roosevelt administration's shameful decision in June 1939 to turn away the German ocean liner *St. Louis* and its 937 passengers, nearly all of them Jewish, forcing the ship to return to Europe, where a fourth died in the Holocaust.[16]

But Corrie ten Boom would also understand the need for national security. She was fiercely loyal to the queen of the Netherlands and was as upset as anyone when the Dutch military collapsed in the face of Nazi aggression. Corrie knew that among the duties of government were punishing evil and keeping the peace so that we could live peaceful, God-honoring lives (1 Tim. 2:1–2; Rom. 13:4). It is doubtful she would look with favor on anything that would leave the door open for terrorists to attack the innocent in this, her adopted country.

However, it is hard to square these legitimate concerns with recent federal actions to bar the door to thousands of innocent and vulnerable people. By any reasonable estimation, Christian refugees are not a clear and present danger to the republic. Yet in 2018, only 15,748 Christian refugees entered the United States, a 36 percent decline from 2017 and a plunge of 55 percent from 2016. Even worse, according to Open Doors, just 1,215 Christians were resettled from the eleven countries cited as the worst for Christians, a drop of nearly 75 percent from the previous year.[17]

The Hiding Place offers some small but telling clues about what *our* attitude should be toward refugees. At the beginning of the book, Corrie recounts the centennial celebration of the watch business at the Beje. Neighbors of every sort are coming to celebrate with Casper ten Boom.

"All through the short winter afternoon they kept coming, the people who counted themselves Father's friends," she wrote. "Young and old, poor and rich, scholarly gentlemen and illiterate servant girls—only to Father did it seem that they were all alike. That was Father's secret: not that he overlooked differences in people; that he didn't know they were there."[18] Perhaps we could benefit from this same kind of benign ignorance about our neighbors in God's world.

Another clue comes near the end of *The Hiding Place*. Betsie and Corrie are at Ravensbrück, undergoing a Friday medical inspection in an unheated corridor in front of leering guards. The middle-aged women are naked, stripped of both clothing and dignity. "How there could be any pleasure in the sight of these stick-thin legs and bloated stomachs I could not imagine," Corrie wrote. "Surely there is no more wretched sight than the human body unloved and uncared for."[19] Corrie had a heart for exploited and suffering people, having experienced this kind of degradation herself.

Even in the grimmest of circumstances, Corrie saw the dignity of every human being, however wretched his or her condition. Knowing her true home was in heaven, she sought to love and care for such people on the margins, even at great personal risk. Can we, who seek to understand and honor Corrie's legacy, do any less?

CHAPTER 14

THE ELDERLY: CARING FOR THOSE WHO ARE NO LONGER "USEFUL"

From her earliest years, Corrie ten Boom cared for the elderly, and when she grew old, she allowed others to care for her. It's just what Christians did. It's what they must continue to do in our youth-obsessed, utilitarian culture in which respect for the aged is no longer a given.

The Hiding Place is full of people who are well past "their prime." So is the Beje, where readers encounter many of them.

- Mama, Corrie's wise and loving mother, serves neighbors young and old, even on days when she can hardly get out of bed herself.
- Tante Jans is a peripatetic pamphleteer and Christian activist, who slows down only when diabetes forces her.
- Casper ten Boom has no head for business but a commitment to craftsmanship as well as a patient and forgiving heart for just about everyone.

- Pickwick is, even by his own admission, an ugly old man with a love for children and a steely determination to rescue the oppressed.
- Christoffels, one of Father's employees, does his work with care and precision and endures the abuse of a Nazi sympathizer with quiet dignity.
- Corrie and Betsie are unmarried, childless, and in their fifties but are fully employed in the family business and in ministry to many people in Haarlem.

The aged in Corrie's world are not perfect, but more times than not they possess deep wisdom and empathy for others—much of it leavened by a rock-solid trust in God. They are more often than not actively working in what we might call their "retirement years."

And then we come to people whose physical decline allows them to do little that we would consider "productive." Corrie's experiences with these aged ones would sometimes be reflected in her own experience later in life. In 1918, Mama had her major stroke while standing at the sink, with the tap water running over her feet. For the next two months, Cor Luitingh ten Boom lay in a coma on her bed.

When Cor finally awakened, she had lost much of her motor function and most of her speech. The only words Mama retained were "yes," "no," and "Corrie"—a name she used for everyone. Communication therefore was extremely difficult. So she and Corrie devised "a little game, something like Twenty Questions."

Mama would start by speaking Corrie's name, and her daughter would respond by asking questions that received a "yes" or a "no" answer. If it was someone's birthday, for example, Corrie would find out. When the "game" was over, Corrie would write that person a note saying Mama was thinking of her. Then

Corrie would get her mother to sign the note with a scrawling signature before sending it on.[1] It was a painstaking process, full of love and lessons for Corrie.

They were lessons that Corrie would apply to her own life. In her later years, Corrie would tell her ministry partners, friends, and helpers that she hoped she would die with her "boots on." Unlike Tante Jans, she wanted to be busy about her Lord's business until the very end, not felled by poor health. Yet Jesus the Victor had another plan. A series of strokes began in 1978, and in her last five years Corrie was mostly confined to a bed. Her helper for this part of her pilgrimage, Pam Rosewell (later, Moore), called this period Corrie's "five silent years."

Despite her stated desire to die with her "boots on," Corrie (pictured here during her later years at her California home with longtime friend Billy Graham) would serve the Lord in ill health during her "five silent years."

Pam says that she and Corrie worked out a similar system of communication, with Corrie using facial expressions and answering "Ja!" or "Nee!" to simple questions. Corrie, like her mother, could encourage others, learning that she was valuable to God no matter what she was able to accomplish—with or without her "boots on." Corrie was learning the hard but necessary lesson that when the Lord asks his people to love him with all their strength, the measure of that strength is not important. What counts is the attitude of the heart.

It's a lesson that most people, if they are fortunate enough to live that long, must face. Aging and its growing physical limitations are a natural part of human life in a fallen world. Corrie ten Boom experienced them, and chances are that we will too. How should we respond? Corrie's life provides a clue. Pam writes, "She had served Him in her youth; now she was serving Him in her old age. She had served Him in strength, now she was serving Him in weakness. She had served Him in health; she was serving Him in illness. She had served Him in her life; she was serving Him in her death. We saw how God built her up in her spirit daily, did not forsake her, provided for her, and sustained her. A new awe and respect for the preciousness of human life came into our thinking."[2]

Such awe and respect, tragically, are largely missing for the aged in our midst today. With the crumbling of the Judeo-Christian worldview across the Western world, increasingly, old people are seen as burdens on the young or on the rest of society—often by the aged themselves. With health-care costs spiraling, seniors often pick up the subtle message—sometimes not so subtle—that it is time for them to step aside. According to the *Journal of the American Medical Association*, between 0.3 percent and 4.6 percent of all deaths, depending on the country, are reported as legal euthanasia or physician-assisted suicide. In the Netherlands, there were 5,516 deaths due to euthanasia in 2015, or 3.7 percent of all deaths.[3]

Some who choose to end their lives do so because they do not want to experience the pain associated with their illnesses (even though palliative care often can make them more comfortable, as it did for Corrie). Others choose to die because of a perceived loss of autonomy and dignity and being less able to enjoy life's activities.[4] In some circumstances, it's not clear that those who die by a physician's hand actually have chosen to do so.

Washington Post opinion writer Charles Lane reports on a growing trend of involuntary euthanasia in Corrie's Netherlands, where physician-assisted suicide has been legal since 1984. He describes the case of a seventy-four-year-old woman, designated in official documents only as "2016-85." She had made an advance directive for euthanasia in the case of dementia, but the directive was not clearly worded. When the woman was placed in a nursing home, she was unable to clarify what she wanted. Her husband, however, requested that she be put to death. A lethal injection was prepared. What happened next was horrifying: "To ensure the patient's compliance, the doctor gave her coffee spiked with a sedative, and, when the woman still recoiled from the needle, asked family members to hold her down. After 15 minutes were spent by the doctor trying to find a vein, the lethal infusion flowed."[5]

Euthanasia, of course, was practiced against "undesirables" in Nazi Germany even before the war. According to one estimate, between 1939 and 1945, German doctors killed more than two hundred thousand disabled people, including infants and the mentally disabled.[6] Today the practice has returned and is legal in Holland, Belgium, Switzerland, Colombia, and the state of Oregon. Will we allow the horror to spread even further?

No doubt Corrie ten Boom would not understand. In *The Hiding Place* she noted the ugly mistreatment of the old clock-mender Christoffels by one of Father's employees, a contemptuous German named Otto. Willem told his incredulous father that such bullying was a natural outgrowth of Nazi ideology, saying, "It's the old and the weak who are to be eliminated."[7]

Reflecting on Corrie's example when this strong woman of God was old and weak, Pam noted that many of us see the elderly merely through a utilitarian lens. For many years past her "prime," Corrie was productive indeed—ministering in sixty-three countries, writing more than thirty books, speaking to prisoners and refugees, forgiving her enemies, founding a ministry, befriending the famous and the unknown, making movies, and much more. But Corrie ten Boom was no less precious to her friends, and to her Lord, when confined to her sickbed.

Given all this, Pam suggested a question that we all should consider in light of Corrie's pilgrimage: "Is human life valuable?"[8] If Christians agree that it is, then several more questions follow. Will we care for the old and weak among us? Will we honor our elderly, as Corrie did for her father, and as Pam and others did for her—doing all in our power to acknowledge their inherent dignity, even when they are no longer "useful" to us?

It's what Christians do.

—

CHAPTER 15

THE THIRD RAIL: SHARING THE GOOD NEWS WITH JEWS

Evidence that Corrie ten Boom shared the Good News with Jewish people, or believed that they needed a Savior, is slight in *The Hiding Place*. Yet her commitment to telling God's chosen people about Jesus their Messiah is undeniable.

She once described one of her family's Haarlem neighbors, Harry de Vries, as "a Christian . . . without ceasing in the least to be a loyal Jew. 'A completed Jew,' he would tell us smilingly. 'A follower of the one perfect Jew.'"[1]

K. Alan Snyder notes that the family "disagreed with the Jewish rejection of Jesus as the Messiah, but sought to love them into what they considered to be the fulfillment of the promises originally made to the Chosen People."[2] This love was manifested in a gentle sharing of the Good News in word and deed. "Willem didn't try to change people," Corrie remarked, "just to serve them."[3]

One of Corrie's acts of service to her Jewish neighbors during the war led to an evangelism opportunity during the fifties in

Australia. Pamela Rosewell Moore tells about the encounter in her book *Life Lessons from the Hiding Place*. She quotes Corrie:

> While in Melbourne I met a Dutchman from my own hometown of Haarlem, who asked me, "Do you remember that thirteen years ago you sent me a Jewish baby of two weeks old?"
>
> "No," I answered, "I only remembered that there were a hundred babies from a Jewish [o]rphanage and that we distributed them to a hundred families, but I really do not remember to whom I sent them."
>
> "Well, here is one of them," he answered, and before me stood Martin, a lovely boy. He looked with interest at the Dutch lady who had saved his life thirteen years before. A bit later I had the great joy of bringing him to a decision for the Lord Jesus.
>
> Next day in school he gave his first testimony, "Boys," he said, "yesterday I met the lady who saved my life when I was two weeks old, and boys, listen. I think I will be a good boy now, for she has told me how to ask Jesus to come into my heart, and He will make me good."[4]

While *The Hiding Place* provides scant evidence of Corrie's attempts to point Jews to Jesus (other than through her loving example), a story of a chance encounter with a Jewish woman in Schveningen Prison survives in her earlier, self-written account, *A Prisoner and Yet* . . . . While Corrie was in her cell alone, a Jewish woman was suddenly pushed inside. Corrie said her new cell partner was friendly but "greatly distressed and worried," particularly about her diabetic husband. No doubt Corrie had not forgotten what had happened to Tante Jans.

After the woman was interrogated in Scheveningen, Corrie wrote, she became tormented by the thought of "the transport." Corrie saw this Jewish woman moaning, "Will they torture me to death? Will they put me into the gas chamber?"

"I tried to tell her of God's love," Corrie said, "but she was impervious to comfort. I was not lonely now, but was alone with someone who had given way completely to fear. I prayed constantly for her and struggled with the Lord for her salvation." The Nazis soon took the woman away.[5]

Corrie's willingness to share Jesus with Jews—and with everyone she met—continued long after she was freed by the Nazis. *Tramp for the Lord* recounts her patient evangelism of a Jewish man in Buenos Aires who could not speak and who was dying from polio. Corrie asked him, "But do you know the Jew, Jesus, as your personal Messiah?" Right before the man died, he wrote, "For the first time I prayed in Jesus' name."[6]

Writing to supporters from a Kansas farm in 1946, Corrie recapped some of her recent ministry highlights in America, including a visit to Chicago. She said that a congress of Jewish women there "did not accept me at all and one asked me: 'Did not you know that you were speaking to Jews? Why did you speak of Jesus?' I certainly did."[7]

In 1974 Corrie traveled to Israel to speak at a meeting of charismatic believers and to work with World Wide Pictures on the coming film. While there she apparently suffered a "heart attack," according to a board summary of Christians Inc., but after two days of rest was able to continue. During this trip, Corrie presented the two-millionth copy of *The Hiding Place* to an aide for Prime Minister Golda Meier. "A special time of prayer took place in Miss Meier's office," the board minutes report. "Corrie and Ellen [Stamps] met many Jews and had the opportunity to speak of Jesus to them."[8]

This track record of evangelism, therefore, puts into context Elizabeth Sherrill's conviction that Corrie never sought to convert Jews. "I never heard her once say anything about converting a Jew," she said. "She wanted to share the love of Christ. None of the Jews she helped became Christians. She recognized Christ as the perfect Jew."[9] Yet Corrie's commitment to sharing Jesus with other Jews—not so that they could become "Christians" but "completed" Jews—was undeniable.

Corrie did not focus on Jewish evangelism in her ministry. At one point Christians Inc. appeared to step back from anything that could be seen as what some today call "targeting" of Jews for conversion. In June 1976, Pam circulated a proposed statement of purpose, most of it written by Corrie, to Brother Andrew, Walter Gastil, and Bill Butler. According to the document, the focus of Christians Inc. would be to reach as many people as possible with the gospel, to encourage people to love their enemies, to prepare for Jesus's return, and to be filled with the Holy Spirit. Among the ministry initiatives to fulfill this purpose was the following: "Reaching Jewish people with material help and the Gospel."[10] When the statement of purpose was approved the following month, however, those words were gone.[11]

In a July 1976 board meeting of Christians Inc., Corrie also decided that the ministry would not support or endorse any other work involved in Jewish missions. "Since many missions are looked down upon by Jews," the minutes of the meeting read, "and because Corrie has good standing with them, she feels that she has a special mission to the Jews, and therefore should support no other."[12]

While these developments no doubt would be disappointing to reputable, long-standing outreaches such as Jews for Jesus, they did not necessarily represent a lessened commitment to sharing Jesus with Jews. They may instead have indicated a strategic decision to emphasize the love of God with *all* people, and not just Jews. This nuanced approach would allow the work to go on without stirring up undue controversy, which might hinder the reception of her message of forgiveness through Jesus the Victor.

If so, Corrie would be following in some famous footsteps. Years before, Billy Graham had decided that he would not "single out the Jews as Jews" in his evangelistic efforts, even though as a leader in the Lausanne movement he was in a sense the spiritual grandfather of the Lausanne Consultation on Jewish Evangelism. Indeed, the evangelist went so far as to distance himself from outreaches focused on Jews in 1973 and in 2000. "As early as the 1957 New York crusade," *Christianity Today* reported, "Graham explained that his strategy did not involve recruiting people out of their religious families: 'Anyone who makes a decision at our meetings is seen later and referred to a local clergyman, Protestant, Catholic, or Jewish.'"[13]

While Corrie would continue speaking of her Savior to God's chosen people off and on during her decades of international prominence, perhaps her greatest opportunity would come in the very heart of the Jewish world on February 28, 1968—twenty-four years to the day that she was arrested at the Beje. The Israeli government had asked her to come to Jerusalem to plant a tree in the Garden of the Righteous at Yad Vashem, the tiny nation's Holocaust memorial, in honor of Corrie and her family's work saving Jews during World War II.

"How the Lord gave me an opportunity to bring the Gospel to many Jews in an official position who were present," Corrie told supporters, "just by telling about my family."[14] What follows is an edited and shortened portion of her remarks that sunny but solemn day.

It is 24 years ago today that I was arrested together with my old father, my whole family and many of my friends. It was in 1844 that my grandfather started in his watchmakers shop a weekly prayer meeting for the peace of Jerusalem and for the salvation and the happiness of the Jews. God gave a divine but understandable answer to that prayer. A hundred years later in that very same house, grandfather's son, four of his grandchildren and a great-grandson were arrested, because they had saved Jews. Four of them had the honor to be martyred for the beloved people of Israel, for they died in prison. I myself have suffered in three prisons.

The love for the Jews was in our blood, in our hearts. When I was a child I once asked my brother: "Why do we love the Jews so very much?"

"Well, Corrie, they are God's chosen people."

"But there are Jews that do not love God."

"That is true, but when I ask a girl to marry me, she must choose me too, before things are all right between us. The Jews are God's chosen people, but they themselves must say 'yes' to the Lord."

I remember that Nollie said to me: "We love the Jews because we have to thank them for the two greatest riches that we have. First, a Book, written by Jews. We must thank them for the Bible, a book almost bursting with Good News. Only the writer Luke was not a Jew, but he was converted by a Jew." The second great blessing that Nollie mentioned was that our greatest Friend Jesus is a Jew. He was after His divine side the Son of God, but after His human side He was a Jew.

This Friend, this Savior Jesus, has been with me. When I was in that horrible concentration camp, He never left me alone. Here in Yad Vashem, I thank you, Israel, for these riches.

Once, Betsie said to me: "Corrie, God spoke to me this night. When we are free, we have a task. We must travel over the world, we must tell the people what we learned here. I have always believed, but now I know from experience, that Jesus' light is stronger than the deepest darkness. When people will say: 'Oh, but your faith has carried you through this prison experience,' we can tell them how weak, how wavering our faith was. No, it was Jesus, our greatest Friend, who has carried us through."

"Corrie, never tell people that it was your faith, for people will say, 'I haven't got Corrie ten Boom's faith.' But when you tell people that it was Jesus, then they will know that the same Jesus who carried us through is willing to carry them through also. For Jesus died at the cross for the sins of the whole world, not only for us, but for all the Jews and the Gentiles of the world, and He says, 'Come unto Me, all who are heavy laden.' So we have a message for the whole world."

Many of you who are here expect the Messiah, and we Christians do too. We know that He has promised: "I will come and I will make everything anew." And then this world will be covered with the knowledge of God like the waters cover the bottom of the sea.

Hallelujah! The best is yet to be! I wish you Shalom, Shalom![15]

Corrie ten Boom, whether speaking to Jew or Gentile, in her life and in her ministry, had a message of faith, hope, and love in the victorious Jewish Messiah. In his constant care, she had lived an imperfect but victorious life—in her decades of preparation, in her short but life-changing months of persecution, in her decades of growing prominence, and in her quiet pilgrimage finally out of the spotlight.

In Jesus the *Overwinnaar* she had found her own hiding place.

Acknowledgments

"Every experience God gives us," Corrie ten Boom once said, "every person He puts in our lives is the perfect preparation for a future that only He can see."[1] You will see the truth of Corrie's statement when you read her modern Christian classic, *The Hiding Place*. You will also note it, I hope, as you read this book.

This volume came upon the author unawares, when he was minding his own business. Unknown to him, a friend and associate, Jerry Root, had recommended him for this project about one of evangelical Christianity's most revered recent historical figures. After you read it, you will have a better vantage point from which to judge the wisdom of Jerry's confidence in said author. Thank you, Jerry.

The author flung himself into the research and writing of this book with gusto but with little more than a rudimentary grasp of its subject. More than a few kind and knowledgeable people helped him get up to speed. They include, in no particular order, the following people:

The expert and incredibly helpful team at the wonderfully convenient (and desperately needed) Billy Graham Center Archives at Wheaton College. Thank you, especially, Bob Shuster, Katherine Graber, and Keith Call.

Elizabeth Sherrill. She provided the author with a vital living connection to Corrie. Tibby, as her friends call her, was extremely patient as she responded to the author's repeated phone calls and emails on some often confusing (at least to the author) historical details. Her insights pepper this book's pages. Thank you, Mrs. Sherrill (or is it Tibby?).

Pam Rosewell Moore. Another close connection to Corrie. This volume would not be nearly so detailed without her prior painstaking research and thoughtful comments during our interview. Thank you, Pam.

Larry Eskridge. His knowledge of the 1970s and where *The Hiding Place* fits into the evangelical subculture, and kindness in sharing it, was invaluable. Thank you, Larry.

Al Janssen. Al is a writer as well as a friend and associate of Brother Andrew. Al generously provided not only useful documents and insights for the book; he also offered sage advice on navigating through some potentially sticky issues. Thank you, Al.

John Wilson. Though he rarely appears in these pages, his suggestions early on in the research and interviewing phase cast a bright and clarifying light on the final product. Thank you, John.

Verne Becker and Mickey Maudlin. For their journalistic sleuthing on a couple of small but critical points. Thank you, Verne and Mickey.

Shaun Tabatt. For the number. Thank you, Shaun.

Rita Mayell. Her description of a chance encounter with Corrie in a lady's restroom is priceless. Thank you, Rita.

Michelle Rich. For your patience and professional touch. Thank you, Michelle.

Jon Sweeney. For trusting Jerry and for your deft suggestions throughout. Thank you, Jon.

The Billy Graham Evangelistic Association. For the lovely photos. Thank you.

Christine. You know why. Thank you, Sweetheart.

As always, any errors or omissions are the responsibility of the author. May those offended by them forgive him as readily as Corrie undoubtedly would.

Notes

Chapter 1: A Dizzying Era

1   Endorsements taken from Corrie ten Boom's *The Hiding Place* (Grand Rapids, MI: Chosen, 2006).

2   "Inaugural Address of President John F. Kennedy," Washington, DC, John F. Kennedy Library, January 20, 1961, https://www.jfklibrary.org/Research/Research-Aids/Ready-Reference/JFK-Quotations/Inaugural-Address.aspx.

3   Definition taken from the National Association of Evangelicals, "What Is an Evangelical?," accessed May 14, 2019, https://www.nae.net/what-is-an-evangelical/.

4   National Association of Evangelicals, "What Is an Evangelical?"

5   For example, William Wilberforce, an evangelical parliamentarian born in 1759, was instrumental in the abolition of the British slave trade. Wilberforce also worked on a wide array of other issues. According to the BBC, "Wilberforce's other efforts to 'renew society' included the organisation of the Society for the Suppression of Vice in 1802. He worked with the reformer, Hannah More, in the Association for the Better Observance of Sunday. Its goal was to provide all children with regular education in reading, personal hygiene and religion. He was closely involved with the Royal Society for the Prevention of Cruelty to Animals. He was also instrumental in encouraging Christian missionaries to go to India." See "William Wilberforce (1759–1833)," BBC, accessed May 14, 2019, ttp://www.bbc.co.uk/history/historic_figures/wilberforce_william. shtml.

6   Luke 10:25–37.

7   Justin Taylor, "A Conversation with Four Historians on the Response of White Evangelicals to the Civil Rights Movement," The Gospel Coalition, July 1, 2016, https://www.thegospelcoalition.org/blogs/evangelical-history/a-conversation-with-four-historians-on-the-response-of-white-evangelicals-to-the-civil-rights-movement/.

8   Lon Allison, *Billy Graham: An Ordinary Man and His Extraordinary God* (Brewster, MA: Paraclete Press, 2018), 101.

9   Steven P. Miller, *Billy Graham and the Rise of the Republican South* (Philadelphia: University of Pennsylvania Press, 2011); quoted in Ray Nothstine, Acton Institute, "'Billy Graham and the Rise of the Republican South,'" *Religion and Liberty* 20, no. 1 (July 20, 2010): https://acton.org/ billy-graham-and-rise-republican-south.

10   Grant Wacker, *America's Pastor: Billy Graham and the Shaping of a Nation* (Cambridge: Belknap Press, 2014), 426; quoted in Allison, *Billy Graham*, 104.

11   Leslie Kramer, "How the Great Inflation of the 1970s Happened," *Investopedia*, updated February 7, 2018, https://www.investopedia.com/articles/economics/09/1970s-great-inflation.asp.

12   "OPEC Oil Embargo, Its Causes, and the Effects of the Crisis," *The Balance*, updated February 20, 2018, https://www.thebalance.com/opec-oil-embargo-causes-and-effects-of-the-crisis-3305806.

13   David Frum, *How We Got Here: The '70s* (New York: Basic Books, 2000), 318.

14   Joseph Patrick Hobbs, Dwight D. Eisenhower, and George Catlett Marshall, *Dear General: Eisenhower's Wartime Letters to Marshall* (Baltimore: Johns Hopkins University Press, 1999), 223; quoted in "Holocaust Denial," Wikipedia, accessed May 14, 2019, https://en.wikipedia.org/wiki/Holocaust_denial#cite_note-30.

15   "Antisemitism in the United States," Wikipedia, accessed May 14, 2019, https://en.wikipedia.org/wiki/Antisemitism_in_the_United_States.

16   Frank Newport, "This Christmas, 78% of Americans Identify as Christian," Gallup, December 24, 2009, https://news.gallup.com/poll/124793/this-christmas-78-americans-identify-christian.aspx.

17   Peter J. Duignan, "Making and Remaking America: Immigration into the United States," Hoover Institution, September 15, 2003, https://www.hoover.org/research/making-and-remaking-america-immigration-united-states.

18   Jonathan Merritt, "Defining 'Evangelical,'" *The Atlantic*, December 7, 2015, https://www.theatlantic.com/politics/archive/2015/12/evangelical-christian/418236/.

Chapter 2: Religion, Jews, and the "Evil Empire"

1   "Inaugural Address of President John F. Kennedy," Washington, DC, John F. Kennedy Library, January 20, 1961, https://www.jfklibrary.org/Research/Research-Aids/Ready-Reference/JFK-Quotations/Inaugural-Address.aspx.

2   "Introduction," Dwight D. Eisenhower Library, Abilene, Kansas, accessed May 14, 2019, https://www.eisenhower.archives.gov/research/subject_guides/pdf/Eisenhower_Religion.pdf, citing Stephen J. Whitfield, *The Culture of the Cold War* (Baltimore: The Johns Hopkins University Press, 1991).

3   "Christianism vs. Communism," Billy Graham Evangelistic Association, Minneapolis, Minnesota, 1951, https://billygraham.org/audio/christianism-vs-communism/.

4   Ronald Reagan, "Evil Empire Speech," March 8, 1983, Voices of Democracy, http://voicesofdemocracy.umd.edu/reagan-evil-empire-speech-text/.

5   "God in the White House," Dwight Eisenhower, *God in America*, Public Broadcasting Service, http://www.pbs.org/godinamerica/god-in-the-white house/.

6   Brother Andrew, with John and Elizabeth Sherrill, *God's Smuggler* (GrandRapids, MI: Chosen, 2015).

7   "Brother Andrew's Story," Open Doors, accessed May 14,2019, https://www.opendoorsusa.org/about-us/history/broth- er-andrews-story/?keyword=god%27s%20smugler&e&g&238243439006&1t1&c&101 2341245&53841882870&g- clid=CjwKCAjwqarbBRBtEiwArlfEIEZUPSOY lV2FJ4zQBrKm2Iu5BqCINS-34GzMbbbVVXI_pFVNQPfhIkxoCfYwQAvD_BwE.

8   See, for example, Stan Guthrie, "The Ten Best Books I've Ever Read," Break-Point, June 7, 2018, http://www.breakpoint.org/2018/06/ten-best-books-ive-ever-read/.

9   Open Doors, "Brother Andrew's Story." Wikipedia, however, puts the number of copies sold by 2016 at 17 million (see note 8 in "Andrew van der Bijl," accessed May 14, 2019, https://en.wikipedia.org/wiki/Andrew_van_der_Bijl).

10   Larry Eskridge, email to the author, June 13, 2018.

11 Larry Eskridge, email to the author, June 13, 2018.
12 Larry Eskridge, God's Forever Family: The Jesus People Movement in America (Oxford: Oxford University Press, 2013).
13 Adapted from the book description on Amazon.com, accessed May 14, 2019, https://www.amazon.com/Gods-Forever-Family-Movement-America/dp/0195326458.
14 Ruth Tucker, "Remembering Moishe Rosen," *Christianity Today*, May 21, 2010, https://www.christianitytoday.com/ct/2010/mayweb-only/30-52.0.html.
15 Larry Eskridge, email to the author, June 13, 2018.
16 Pietism was a reformed movement that began in the seventeenth-century German Lutheran Church, emphasizing a strong personal faith and adherence to biblical doctrine. Corrie ten Boom, who was Dutch, was a member of the Dutch Reformed Church. As an adult after the war she was later rebaptized in a Baptist church in India.
17 Larry Eskridge, email to the author, June 13, 2018.

Chapter 3: A Book Is Lived

1   "Isaac Da Costa, 'I Realized the Fulfilment of the Prophecies' (1798–1860)," Jewish Testimonies (several spellings changed to American English style), accessed May 14, 2019, https://www.jewishtestimonies.com/en/isaac-da-costa-realised-fulfilment-prophecies-1798-1860/.
2   Corrie ten Boom, *Father ten Boom: God's Man* (Grand Rapids, MI: Fleming H. Revell, 1978), 29, 31–33; quoted in Pamela Rosewell Moore, *Life Lessons from the Hiding Place: Discovering the Heart of Corrie ten Boom* (Minneapolis: Chosen, 2004), 195–96.
3   Moore, *Life Lessons*, 197.
4   Moore, *Life Lessons*, 206.
5   Moore, *Life Lessons*, 197.
6   Moore, *Life Lessons*, 206–7.
7   Elizabeth Sherrill, "The Hiding Place," accessed May 14, 2019, https://www.elizabethsherrill.com/the-hiding-place-book-desc.html.
8   Moore, *Life Lessons*, 50.
9   Corrie ten Boom, *The Hiding Place* (Grand Rapids, MI: Chosen, 2006), 21.
10 One example: Corrie's publisher placed three of her earlier devotional works—*He Cares, He Comforts*, on sickness and affliction; *He Sets the Captive Free*, on forgiveness; and *Don't Wrestle, Just Nestle*, on emotional distress—between the covers of one book: *Jesus Is Victor* (Grand Rapids, MI: Fleming H. Revell,1985). Jesus the Victor was a constant theme in Corrie's spiritual life, one she consistently shared with others.
11 Gustaf Aulèn, *Christus Victor: An Historical Study of the Three Main Types of the Idea of Atonement* (repr., Eugene, OR: Wipf and Stock, 1931), 20.
12 "Peter Paul Rubens: Christus als overwinnaar van Satan en de Dood, 1618–1622," Nederlands Instituut voor Kunstgeschiedenis, accessed May 14, 2019, https://rkd.nl/nl/explore/images/265592
13 Collection 78 Papers of Corrie ten Boom, 1902–1997, Billy Graham Center Archives, Wheaton College, https://archon.wheaton.edu/?p=collections/finding-aid&id=1281&q=&rootcontentid=269814#scopecontent.
14 Ten Boom, *Father ten Boom*, 102–3.

15 Moore, *Life Lessons*, 207–9.
16 Ten Boom, *Hiding Place*, 29.
17 Ten Boom, *Hiding Place*, 29–30.
18 Ten Boom, *Hiding Place*, 27–31.
19 Ten Boom, *Hiding Place*, 40.
20 Ten Boom, *Hiding Place*, 41–42.
21 Ten Boom, *Hiding Place*, 43–44.
22 Ten Boom, *Hiding Place*, 56–60.
23 Elizabeth Sherrill, preface, in Ten Boom, *Hiding Place*, 13.
24 Ten Boom, *Hiding Place*, 32.
25 Ten Boom, *Hiding Place*, 79.
26 Suzanne Burden, "Meet the Dutch Christians Who Saved Their Jewish Neighbors from the Nazis," *Christianity Today*, November 23, 2015, https://www.christianitytoday.com/ct/2015/december/meet-dutch-christians-saved-their-jewish-neighbors-nazis.html.
27 Ten Boom, *Hiding Place*, 85.
28 Ten Boom, *Hiding Place*, 81–87.
29 Ten Boom, *Hiding Place*, 88–89.
30 Corrie ten Boom, *A Prisoner and Yet . . .* (repr., Fort Washington, PA: CLC Publications, 2018), 9.
31 Ten Boom, *Hiding Place*, 90.
32 Ten Boom, *Hiding Place*, 93–94.
33 Ten Boom, *Hiding Place*, 94–103.
34 Ten Boom, *Prisoner*, 19.
35 Ten Boom, *Hiding Place*, 152.
36 "Ravensbrück," *Holocaust Encyclopedia*, United States Holocaust Memorial Museum, accessed May 14, 2019, https://www.ushmm.org/wlc/en/article.php?ModuleId=10005199.
37 "The Hiding Place," Corrie ten Boom Online Archive, Dallas Baptist University, accessed May 14, 2019, https://www3.dbu.edu/corrie-ten-boom/the-hiding-place.htm.
38 Ten Boom, *Hiding Place*, 227.

Chapter 4: A Communicator Is Born

1 "Bombing of Darmstadt in World War II," Wikipedia, accessed May 14, 2019, https://en.wikipedia.org/wiki/Bombing_of_Darmstadt_in_World_War_II.
2 See website of George Faithful, accessed May 14, 2019, http://georgefaithful.com/about/.
3 George Faithful, "The Evangelical Sisterhood of Mary: Profile of a Protestant Monastic Order," 1, accessed May 14, 2019, http://georgefaithful.com/wp-content/uploads/2011/04/Evangelical-Sisterhood.pdf.
4 Faithful, "The Evangelical Sisterhood of Mary," 1.
5 Faithful, "The Evangelical Sisterhood of Mary," 3.
6 Faithful, "The Evangelical Sisterhood of Mary," 4.
7 Elizabeth Sherrill, preface, in Corrie ten Boom, *The Hiding Place* (Grand Rapids, MI: Chosen, 2006), 11.
8 Elizabeth Sherrill, interview with the author, August 17, 2018.
9 Elizabeth Sherrill, interview with the author, August 17, 2018.
10 "John and Elizabeth Sherrill," Wikipedia, accessed May 14, 2019, https://en.wikipedia.org/wiki/John_and_Elizabeth_Sherrill.

11   The account of this meeting is taken from two sources: an interview with Elizabeth Sherrill by the author on May 30, 2018, and Elizabeth Sherrill, preface, in Ten Boom, *Hiding Place*, 11.

12   Elizabeth Sherrill, preface, in Ten Boom, *Hiding Place*, 11–12.

13   Corrie ten Boom, *A Prisoner and Yet . . .* (repr., Fort Washington, PA: CLC Publications, 2018), 45.

14   Pamela Rosewell Moore, *Life Lessons from the Hiding Place: Discovering theHeart of Corrie ten Boom* (Minneapolis: Chosen, 2004), 81–82.

15   Moore, *Life Lessons*, 84.

16   Elizabeth Sherrill, interview with the author, May 30, 2018.

17   Moore, *Life Lessons*, 114.

18   Moore, *Life Lessons*, 114.

19   Moore, *Life Lessons*, 117–18.

20   Ten Boom, *Hiding Place*, 34.

21   Ten Boom, *Hiding Place*, 50–51.

22   Ten Boom, *Hiding Place*, 54–55.

23   Corrie ten Boom, *Amazing Love: True Stories of the Power of Forgiveness* (repr., Fort Washington, PA: CLC Publications, 2018), 37-41.

24   Corrie ten Boom, *In My Father's House* (Eureka, MT: Lighthouse Trails Publishing, 2011), 72.

25   From a sign of dedication at the church building, dated April 29, 1972, from Google Maps, accessed January 24, 2019.

26   From a photo courtesy of Carey Baptist Church, Ixigo, accessed May 14, 2019, https://www.ixigo.com/carey-baptist-church-kolkata-india-ne-1359200.

27   Moore, *Life Lessons*, 144–45.

28   Michael Maudlin, interview with Brother Andrew, "Conversations: God's Smuggler Confesses," *Christianity Today*, December 11, 1995, https://www .christianitytoday.com/ct/1995/december11/5te045.html.

29   Andrew van der Bijl, untitled, undated tribute in honor of Corrie ten Boom, 1, Collection 78 Papers of Corrie ten Boom, 1902–1997, Billy Graham CenterArchives, Wheaton College.

30   Brother Andrew, "Stories About Corrie ten Boom," supplied by Al Janssen, May 12, 2018.

31   Sam Wellman, *Corrie ten Boom: World War II Heroine* (Uhrichsville, OH: Barbour, 1995), 186.

32   Collection 78 Papers of Corrie ten Boom, 1902–1997, Billy Graham CenterArchives, Wheaton College.

33   "The Light from Billy Graham," *Chicago Tribune*, June 26, 2005, http:// articles.chicagotribune.com/2005-06-26/news/0506260470_1_rev-billy -graham-crusade-preacher.

34   Moore, *Life Lessons*, 153.

35   Pam Rosewell Moore, "Profiles in Faith: Corrie ten Boom (1892–1983)," *Knowing & Doing*, C. S. Lewis Institute, Fall 2004, http://www.cslewisinstitute .org/webfm_send/432.

36   Ten Boom, *Hiding Place*, 247–48.

Chapter 5: A Story Is Retold

1 Rick Hamlin, "In Fond and Grateful Remembrance: John Sherrill," *Guideposts* (web exclusive), December 4, 2017, https://www.guideposts.org/inspiration/inspiring-stories/stories-of-faith/in-fond-and-grateful-remembrance-john-sherrill.

2 Hamlin, "In Fond and Grateful Remembrance."

3 Elizabeth Sherrill, interview with the author, May 30, 2018.

4 Elizabeth Sherrill, interview with the author, May 30, 2018.

5 Elizabeth Sherrill, email to the author, July 1, 2018.

6 Pamela Rosewell Moore, interview with the author, May 22, 2018.

7 The published record of how the Sherrills learned of Corrie and the recollections of Elizabeth Sherrill today are in conflict at certain points. The 1974 edition of *The Hiding Place* from Bantam Books contains a preface by Elizabeth and John Sherrill that says: "When we were doing the research for *God's Smuggler*, a name kept cropping up: Corrie ten Boom. This Dutch lady—in her mid-70s when we first heard of her—was Brother Andrew's favorite traveling companion. . . . His fascinating stories about her in Vietnam, where she had earned that most honorable title 'Double-old Grandmother'—and in a dozen other Communist countries—came to mind so often that we finally had to hold up our hands to stop his flow of reminiscence. 'We could never fit her into the book,' we said. 'She sounds like a book in herself'" (vii). When asked about this, Elizabeth Sherrill said, "I certainly remember Andrew regaling us with Corrie stories, but only after we'd started working with her. I trust my memory here because I still recall the surprise I felt, when I started to give my bona fides to Corrie in Darmstadt, to discover that she already knew our name and reputation." Elizabeth Sherrill further insists that John Sherrill was not present at her first meeting with Corrie (Elizabeth Sherrill, email to the author, September 7, 2018). See also, for example, Corrie's newsletter, *It's Harvest Time* 53 (August 1971): 14: "The Sherrills first heard about Corrie when they were working with Brother Andrew on his book [*God's Smuggler*]. That meeting cast the die for this book." The author believes Elizabeth Sherrill's current recollections to be accurate but cannot speculate as to why there are countervailing accounts in the previously published record other than to suggest that mistakes sometimes happen and then are perpetuated. The reader, of course, is free to come to his or her own conclusions.

8 Elizabeth Sherrill, email to the author, July 1, 2018.

9 Verne Becker, email to the author, August 29, 2018.

10 *It's Harvest Time* (December 1970): 12.

11 *It's Harvest Time* 52 (April 1971): 19.

12 J. R. R. Tolkien, *The Hobbit: Or, There and Back Again* (New York: HoughtonMifflin, 2001), 57.

13 Elizabeth Sherrill, interview with the author, May 30, 2018.

14 Elizabeth Sherrill, interview with the author, May 30, 2018.

15 Elizabeth Sherrill, "Working with Corrie," accessed May 14, 2019, https://www.elizabethsherrill.com/working-with-corrie.html.

16 Moore, *Life Lessons*, 25.

17 Collection 78 Papers of Corrie ten Boom, 1902–1997, Billy Graham CenterArchives, Wheaton College.

18 Moore, *Life Lessons*, 27.

19 Elizabeth Sherrill, interview with the author, May 30, 2018.
20 Corrie ten Boom, *A Prisoner and Yet . . .* (repr., Fort Washington, PA: CLC Publications, 2018), 13.
21 Ten Boom, *Prisoner,* 24.
22 *It's Harvest Time* 53 (August 1971): 14.
23 Elizabeth Sherrill, interview with the author, May 30, 2018.
24 Elizabeth Sherrill, interview with the author, May 30, 2018.
25 Elizabeth Sherrill, interview with the author, May 30, 2018.
26 *It's Harvest Time* 53 (August 1971): 14.
27 "The Hiding Place," *It's Harvest Time* 54 (January 1972):

Chapter 6: Anne and Corrie

1 Larry Eskridge, email to the author, June 13, 2018.
2 Larry Eskridge, email to the author, June 13, 2018.
3 Anne Frank, *Anne Frank: The Diary of a Young Girl* (New York: Doubleday / Bantam, 1967, 1993), 158.
4 Afterword, *Anne Frank,* 279.
5 Afterword, *Anne Frank,* 280.
6 Afterword, *Anne Frank,* 281.
7 Elizabeth Sherrill, interview with the author, August 17, 2018.
8 Afterword, *Anne Frank,* 282.
9 Tom Williams, "The Hiding Place," *Chicago Critic,* accessed May 15, 2019, http://chicagocritic.com/the-hiding-place/.

Chapter 7: On the Silver Screen

1 *It's Harvest Time* 54, "The Hiding Place," January 1972, 8.
2 "Biography," Collection 78 Papers of Corrie ten Boom, 1902–1997, Billy Graham Center Archives, Wheaton College, https://www2.wheaton.edu/bgc /archives/guides/078.htm.
3 Pamela Rosewell Moore, *Life Lessons from the Hiding Place: Discovering the Heart of Corrie ten Boom* (Minneapolis: Chosen, 2004), 176; Corrie ten Boom, *The Hiding Place* (Grand Rapids, MI: Chosen, 2006), "Ten Boom Family Timeline," 264.
4 Rita Mayell, emails to the author, October 27 and October 29, 2018.
5 Billy Graham, *Just as I Am: The Autobiography of Billy Graham* (repr., New York: HarperCollins, 2018), 434; quoted by Janet Chismar, "WWII Heroine Corrie ten Boom Impacts New Generation," Billy Graham Evangelistic Association, April 15, 2010, https://billygraham.org/story/corrie-ten-boom -impacts-new-generation/. The Billy Graham Evangelistic Association did not respond to the author's repeated requests for clarification.
6 In a September 3, 2018, email to the author, Elizabeth Sherrill stated, "I affirm again that Ruth never spoke to me about Corrie, at least not before the book was published. After that, as you know, the Billy Graham organization did the film based on the book. Ruth and I may well have talked about Corrie during that filming. Both of us loved her and I'm sure had Corrie-stories to regale each other with."
7 Billy Graham Evangelistic Association, World Wide Pictures, accessed May 15, 2019, https://billygraham.org/tv-and-radio/worldwide-pictures/.

8   Peter T. Chattaway, "Billy Graham Goes to the Movies," *Patheos*, August 23,2005, http://www.patheos.com/blogs/filmchat/2005/08/billy-graham-goes -to-the-movies.html.
9   Chattaway, "Billy Graham Goes to the Movies."
10   Moore, *Life Lessons*, 177.
11   "Father Settles for $35,000 In Drug Death of Daughter," *New York Times*, July16, 1964, 12, https://www.nytimes.com/1964/07/16/archives/father-settles -for-35000-in-drug-death-of-daughter.html.
12   Collection 78 Papers of Corrie ten Boom, 1902–1997, Billy Graham Center Archives, Wheaton College.
13   Transcript of the Conclusion of the July 21, 1974, Plenary Session of the International Congress on World Evangelization, Collection 78 Papers of Corrie ten Boom, 1902–1997, Billy Graham Center Archives, Wheaton College, https://www2.wheaton.edu/bgc/archives/docs/cn053t012t013a.htm.
14   Walter G. Gastil, "Repost of Status of The Hiding Place Motion Picture, as of September 1, 1975," 1, Christians Incorporated, Collection 78 Papers of Corrie ten Boom, 1902–1997, Billy Graham Center Archives, Wheaton College.
15   "Fullerton, California," Wikipedia, accessed May 15, 2019, https:// en.wikipedia.org/wiki/Fullerton,_California.
16   Gastil, "Repost," 1.
17   Gastil, "Repost," 1.
18   Gastil, "Repost," 2.
19   "The Hiding Place," *It's Harvest Time* 54 (January 1972): 8.
20   Brian Baxter, "Julie Harris Obituary," *The Guardian*, August 25, 2013, https:// www.theguardian.com/stage/2013/aug/25/julie-harris.1
21   "Arthur O'Connell, 73, Nominated for Oscars for Supporting Roles," *New York Times*, May 19, 1981, C00012, https://www.nytimes.com/1981/05/19 /obituaries/arthur-o-connell-73-nominated-for-oscars-for-supporting-roles. html.
22   Ellen de Kroon, "The Hiding Place Film Prayer Letter," undated, Collection 78 Papers of Corrie ten Boom, 1902–1997, Billy Graham Center Archives, Wheaton College.
23   Ellen de Kroon, "The Hiding Place Film Prayer Letter."
24   Gastil, "Repost," 2.
25   Collection 78 Papers of Corrie ten Boom, 1902–1997, Billy Graham Center Archives, Wheaton College.
26   De Kroon, "The Hiding Place Film Prayer Letter."
27   De Kroon, "The Hiding Place Film Prayer Letter."
28   De Kroon, "The Hiding Place Film Prayer Letter."
29   Collection 78 Papers of Corrie ten Boom, 1902–1997, Billy Graham Center Archives, Wheaton College.
30   Gastil, "Subject: Scheduling."
31   Collection 78 Papers of Corrie ten Boom, 1902–1997, Billy Graham Center Archives, Wheaton College.
32   Gastil, "Repost," 1.
33   Steven D. Greydanus, "The Hiding Place (1975)," Decent Films, April 12, 2006,http://decentfilms.com/reviews/hidingplace; reprinted from *National Catholic Register*.
34   Gastil, "Repost," 2.
35   Gastil, "Repost," 3–4.
36   Gastil, "Repost," 2.

37 Rita Mayell, interview with the author, May 16, 2018.

38 In an October 27, 2018, email to the author, Mayell adds, "Several weeks later when the premiere was rescheduled I returned with a friend. I was in my first year of college. For the second time I had an encounter with Corrie. This time she was already in the bathroom washing her hands when I walked in. She faced the mirror looking at me as I stood waiting for a stall. She turned around and pointed and said with such firmness of goal, tenderness, and piercing eyes:'GOOOOOOOOOOOOOOOD LOVES YOU . . .'" She had tears in her eyes. All I remember hearing in the bathroom was silence and 'awes.' It was a holy moment. God stopped time for me, a prodigal who wanted to know Jesus but seemed to not understand how to gain victory. It was a God set up."

39 Mayell interview, and email to the author, October 26, 2018.

40 ten Boom, *Hiding Place*, 266.

41 Graham, *Just as I Am,* quoted in Chismar, "WWII Heroine Corrie ten Boom Impacts New Generation."

42 Graham, *Just as I Am,* quoted in Chismar, "WWII Heroine Corrie ten Boom Impacts New Generation."

43 Graham, *Just as I Am,* quoted in Chismar, "WWII Heroine Corrie ten Boom Impacts New Generation."

44 Graham, *Just as I Am,* quoted in Chismar, "WWII Heroine Corrie ten Boom Impacts New Generation."

45 Lois Armstrong, "Concentration Camp Survivor Corrie Ten Boom Relives Her Grim Story on Film," *People*, December 1, 1975, https://people.com/archive/concentration-camp-survivor-corrie-ten-boom-relives-her-grim-story-on-film- vol-4-no-22/.

Chapter 8: "Keep Looking Down"

1 Brother Andrew, "Stories About Corrie ten Boom," supplied by Al Janssen, May 12, 2018.

2 *The Hiding Place* newsletter, Memorial Edition, Christians Inc., undated, 10, Collection 78 Papers of Corrie ten Boom, 1902–1997, Billy Graham Center Archives, Wheaton College.

3 Walter Gastil, "Minutes of Meeting," Planning and Policy Committee, Christians Inc., September 23, 1975, 1, Collection 78 Papers of Corrie ten Boom, 1902–1997, Billy Graham Center Archives, Wheaton College, slightly edited by author for clarity.

4 Gastil, "Minutes of Meeting," 1.

5 *The Hiding Place* newsletter, Memorial Edition, 10.

6 "Agenda—September 23 Meeting" (1975), Policy and Planning Committee, Christians Inc., 4, Collection 78 Papers of Corrie ten Boom, 1902–1997, Billy Graham Center Archives, Wheaton College.

7 Lois Armstrong, "Concentration Camp Survivor Corrie Ten Boom Relives Her Grim Story on Film," *People*, December 1, 1975, https://people.com/archive/concentration-camp-survivor-corrie-ten-boom-relives-her-grim-story-on-film- vol-4-no-22/.

8 "Board of Directors Meeting," Christians Inc., August 10, 1978, 2, Collection 78 Papers of Corrie ten Boom, 1902–1997, Billy Graham Center Archives, Wheaton College.

9   Gastil, "Minutes of Meeting," 3.
10 Gastil, "Minutes of Meeting," 3.
11 Corrie ten Boom, *The Hiding Place* (Grand Rapids, MI: Chosen, 2006), 266.
12 See website of Corrie ten Boom, accessed May 15, 2019, https://www.corrietenboom.com/en/foundation/organization.
13 Peggy Carter, undated letter to ministry friends, Christians Inc., November 7,1975, Collection 78 Papers of Corrie ten Boom, 1902–1997, Billy Graham Center Archives, Wheaton College.
14 Ten Boom, *Hiding Place*, 266.
15 Corrie ten Boom, untitled letter to Brother Andrew, Christians Inc., November3, 1976, Collection 78 Papers of Corrie ten Boom, 1902–1997, Billy Graham Center Archives, Wheaton College.
16 Pamela Rosewell Moore, *Life Lessons from the Hiding Place: Discovering theHeart of Corrie ten Boom* (Minneapolis: Chosen, 2004), 183.
17 Ten Boom, *Hiding Place*, 265.
18 Brother Andrew, "Stories."
19 Armstrong, "Concentration Camp Survivor Corrie."
20 Corrie ten Boom, untitled document, Christians Inc., February 27, 1979, Collection 78 Papers of Corrie ten Boom, 1902–1997, Billy Graham Center Archives, Wheaton College.
21 Corrie ten Boom, untitled letter to Brother Andrew, November 3, 1976.
22 Corrie ten Boom, untitled letter to ministry supporters, August 8, 1977.

Chapter 9: A Prisoner Once Again
1   Paula Hendrickson, "Rock River Valley Insider: Jane Addams Left a Legacy of Activism," *Rock River Star*, July 21, 2013, http://www.rrstar.com/x853689891/Rock-River-Valley-Insider-Jane-Addams-rose-from-sickbed-to-Nobel-prize.
2   "Minutes, Board Meeting/Dinner," Christians Inc., February 14, 1978, 1, Collection 78 Papers of Corrie ten Boom, 1902–1997, Billy Graham Center Archives, Wheaton College.
3   "Minutes, Board Meeting/Dinner," 1.
4   Pamela Rosewell, *The Five Silent Years of Corrie ten Boom* (Grand Rapids, MI: Zondervan, 1986), 91–92.
5   Rosewell, *Five Silent Years*, 92.
6   See the appendix in the "Ten Boom Family Timeline" in both Pamela Rosewell Moore's *Life Lessons from the Hiding Place: Discovering the Heart of Corrie ten Boom* (Minneapolis: Chosen, 2004) and the 2006 edition of Corrie ten Boom's *The Hiding Place* (Grand Rapids, MI: Chosen, 2006).
7   Rosewell, *Five Silent Years*, 44.
8   See John 21:15–19.
9   This scene is recounted from Rosewell, *Five Silent Years*, 76.

10 Rosewell, *Five Silent Years*, 97–99.
11 Telegram from Billy Butler to Brother Andrew, August 23, 1978, Collection 78 Papers of Corrie ten Boom, 1902–1997, Billy Graham Center Archives, Wheaton College.
12 Pamela Rosewell, "Report to Members of Christians Incorporated Board," undated, 1, Collection 78 Papers of Corrie ten Boom, 1902–1997, Billy Graham Center Archives, Wheaton College.
13 Rosewell, "Report to Members of Christians Incorporated Board," 2.
14 Rosewell, "Report to Members of Christians Incorporated Board," 2.
15 Pamela Rosewell, "A Note from Pamela," *The Hiding Place* newsletter, Memorial Edition, undated, 13, Collection 78 Papers of Corrie ten Boom, 1902–1997, Billy Graham Center Archives, Wheaton College.
16 Rosewell, "Note from Pamela," 13.
17 Rosewell, *Five Silent Years*, 134.
18 Rosewell, *Five Silent Years*, 172.
19 Rosewell, *Five Silent Years*, 185–87.
20 Menachem Posner, "Is It Special to Pass Away on One's Birthday?," Chabad .org, accessed May 15, 2019, https://www.chabad.org/library/article_cdo aid/1452114/jewish/Is-It-Special-to-Pass-Away-on-Ones-Birthday.htm.

Chapter 10: Corrie's Character

1 Pamela Rosewell Moore, interview with the author, May 22, 2018.
2 Brother Andrew, "Stories About Corrie ten Boom," supplied by Al Janssen, May 12, 2018.
3 Corrie ten Boom, *The Hiding Place* (Grand Rapids, MI: Chosen, 2006), 61.
4 Ten Boom, *Hiding Place*, 220.
5 Lois Armstrong, "Concentration Camp Survivor Corrie Ten Boom Relives Her Grim Story on Film," *People*, December 1, 1975, https://people.com/archive/concentration-camp-survivor-corrie-ten-boom-relives-her-grim-story-on-film-vol-4-no-22/.
6 Ten Boom, *Hiding Place*, 215–16.
7 Elizabeth Sherrill, "When Corrie Made Mistakes," accessed May 15, 2019, https://www.elizabethsherrill.com/when-corrie-made-mistakes.html.
8 Sherrill, "When Corrie Made Mistakes."
9 Brother Andrew, letter to "Corrie ten Boom and Committee," February 10,1975, Collection 78 Papers of Corrie ten Boom, 1902–1997, Billy Graham Center Archives, Wheaton College.
10 Andrew van der Bijl, "Corrie ten Boom Book Project for Eastern Europe," September 14, 1977, Collection 78 Papers of Corrie ten Boom, 1902–1997, Billy Graham Center Archives, Wheaton College.
11 Sherrill, "When Corrie Made Mistakes."
12 Pamela Rosewell Moore, *Life Lessons from the Hiding Place: Discovering the Heart of Corrie ten Boom* (Minneapolis: Chosen, 2004), 115–16.
13 See Luke 10:25–37.
14 Corrie ten Boom, *In My Father's House* (Eureka, MT: Lighthouse Trails Publishing, 2011), 181.
15 Elizabeth Sherrill, "Since Then," in Ten Boom, Hiding Place, 251.

Chapter 11: Evangelism: Dispelling the Darkness

1   Ed Stetzer, "America's Age of Skepticism: How Christians Should Respond," *Christianity Today*, September 18, 2018, https://www.christianitytoday .com/edstetzer/2018/september/americas-age-of-skepticism-how-christians -should-respond.html; and "U.S. Public Becoming Less Religious," Pew Research Center, November 3, 2015, http://www.pewforum.org/2015/11/03/ u-s-public-becoming-less-religious/.

2   Suzanne Burden, "Meet the Dutch Christians Who Saved Their Jewish Neighbors from the Nazis," *Christianity Today*, November 23, 2015, https://www .christianitytoday.com/ct/2015/december/meet-dutch-christians-saved-their -jewish-neighbors-nazis.html.

3   "Two-Thirds of People in Netherlands Have No Religious Faith," *DutchNews. nl*, March 14, 2016, https://www.dutchnews.nl/news/2016/03/ two-thirds-of- people-in-netherlands-have-no-religious-faith/.

4   "Sharing Faith Is Increasingly Optional to Christians," Barna Group, May15, 2018, https://www.barna.com/research/sharing-faith-increasingly-optional -christians/.

5   "Sharing Faith."

6   "Sharing Faith."

7   Corrie ten Boom, *The Hiding Place* (Grand Rapids, MI: Chosen, 2006), 114–15.

8   Ten Boom, *Hiding Place*, 174. Pamela Rosewell Moore reports that some years later Corrie visited Hans Rahms in Germany and explained more fully his need for salvation. "I know his sins were forgiven," Corrie said, "and that his name was written in the Book of Life." *Life Lessons from the Hiding Place: Discovering the Heart of Corrie ten Boom* (Minneapolis: Chosen, 2004), 122.

9   Brother Andrew, "Stories About Corrie ten Boom," supplied by Al Janssen, May 12, 2018.

10   Moore, *Life Lessons*, 173–74.

11   Pamela Rosewell, *The Five Silent Years of Corrie ten Boom* (Grand Rapids, MI: Zondervan, 1986), 66.

12   Brother Andrew, "Stories."

13   Rod Dreher, "Could the Catholic Church Collapse?" *The American Conservative*, September 25, 2018, https://www.theamericanconservative.com/ dreher/ could-the-catholic-church-collapse/.

14   John Frederick Walker, *A Certain Curve of Horn: The Hundred-Year Quest for the Giant Sable Antelope of Angola* (New York: Grove Press, 2004), 144; quoted in Doug Ponder, "Are Missionaries Good for the World?" International Mission Board, Southern Baptist Convention, November 8, 2018, https:// www.imb.org/2018/11/08/missionaries-good-for-world/.

15   Andrea Palpant Dilley, "The Surprising Discovery About Those Colonialist, Proselytizing Missionaries," *Christianity Today*, January 8, 2014, https:// www.christianitytoday.com/ct/2014/january-february/world-missionaries -made. html, quoted in Ponder, "Are Missionaries Good for the World?"

Chapter 12: Anti-Semitism: Defending Human Dignity

1   Eric W. Gritsch, "Was Luther Anti-Semitic?" *Christian History* 39 (1993): https://www.christianitytoday.com/history/issues/issue-39/was-luther-anti-semitic.html.

2   David Crary, "Before Shooting, Anti-Semitic Incidents Were on the Rise," AP News, October 29, 2018, https://apnews. com /2d425735493a427ba2aed81300f925eb.

3   Frank Bruni, "The Oldest Hatred, Forever Young," New York Times, April 14, 2014, https://www.nytimes.com/2014/04/15/opinion/the-oldest-hatred-forever -young.html.

4   "Antisemitic Incidents in UK at All-Time High," *The Guardian*, February 1,2018, https://www.theguardian.com/society/2018/feb/01/antisemitic -incidents-in-uk-at-all-time-high.

5   Sue Surkes, "Poll: Most Americans Believe Holocaust Could Happen Again," *Times of Israel*, April 12, 2018, https://www.timesofisrael.com/poll-most -americans-believe-holocaust-could-happen-again/.

6   John Wilson, email to the author, May 18, 2018.

7   Mike Evans, "You Can't Love God Without Loving the Jewish People," Jerusalem Prayer Team, April 10, 2013, https://www.facebook.com/ jerusalemprayerteam/photos/a.10150308507814698/10151867637939698/? type=1&theater.

8   The subject of the final chapter. The article: "Why Evangelize the Jews? God'sChosen People Need Jesus as Much as We Do," *Christianity Today*, March 25, 2008, https://www.christianitytoday.com/ct/2008/march/31.76 .html.

9   Rabbi Yehiel E. Poupko and Stan Guthrie, "Christian Evangelism and Judaism," *Christianity Today*, April 2, 2008, https://www.christianitytoday .com/ct/2008/aprilweb-only/114-33.0.html.

10   See K. Alan Snyder, "Corrie ten Boom: A Protestant Evangelical Response to the Nazi Persecution of Jews: A Paper Presented to the Annual Conference of the Social Science History Association," Chicago, IL, November 1998, 11, https://ponderingprinciples.com/writing/Corrie_ten_Boom.pdf.

11   "Corrie ten Boom," *Holocaust Encyclopedia*, United States Holocaust Memorial Museum, accessed May 15, 2019, https://encyclopedia.ushmm.org/ content/en/article/corrie-ten-boom.

12   Snyder, "Corrie ten Boom," 18.

13   Stan Guthrie, *All That Jesus Asks: How His Questions Can Teach and Transform Us* (Grand Rapids, MI: Baker Books, 2010), 258.

14   Elizabeth Sherrill, "Since Then," in Corrie ten Boom, *The Hiding Place* (Grand Rapids, MI: Chosen, 2006), 252.

Chapter 13: Refugees: Walking with the Sojourners

1   Corrie ten Boom, *The Hiding Place* (Grand Rapids, MI: Chosen, 2006), 240– 42.

2   Ten Boom, *Hiding Place*, 242.

3   Andrew van der Bijl, untitled, undated tribute in honor of Corrie ten Boom, 1902–1997, Billie Graham Center Archives, Wheaton College.

4   Van der Bijl, tribute, 1–2.

5   Van der Bijl, tribute, 1.

6   "Refugee Statistics," UNHCR, accessed May 16, 2019, https://www .unrefugees.org/refugee-facts/statistics/.

7 " "What Is a Refugee?" UNHCR, accessed May 16, 2019, https://www .unrefugees.org/refugee-facts/what-is-a-refugee/.

8 "What Is a Refugee?"

9 "What Is a Refugee?"

10 "Refugee Statistics"; "What Is a Refugee?"

11 "Refugee Statistics."

12 Jennifer Hansler, "US Admits Lowest Number of Refugees in More Than 40Years," CNN, October 2, 2018, https://www.cnn.com/2018/10/02/politics /us- refugees-fy18/index.html.

13 Ten Boom, *Hiding Place*, 262; see also "Bloemendaal 1940–1945," Bloemendaal War Historical Foundation, accessed May 16, 2019, https://1940-1945 .bloemendaal.nl/index.php?id=3, which says Corrie established the home on July 18, 1945.

14 Corrie ten Boom with Jamie Buckingham, *Tramp for the Lord* (New York: Jove Books, 1978), 49–51.

15 Ten Boom, *Hiding Place*, 262.

16 Daniel A. Gross, "The U.S. Government Turned Away Thousands of Jewish Refugees, Fearing That They Were Nazi Spies," *Smithsonian*, November 18, 2015, https://www.smithsonianmag.com/history/us-government-turned -away-thousands-jewish-refugees-fearing-they-were-nazi-spies-180957324/.

17 Griffin Paul Jackson, "No Refuge: Persecuted Christians Entering US Dwindle to Record Low," *Christianity Today*, October 2, 2018, https://www .christianitytoday.com/news/2018/october/persecuted-christians-refugees -entering-us-hits-record-low-.html.

18 Ten Boom, *Hiding Place*, 29.

19 Ten Boom, *Hiding Place*, 207.

Chapter 14: The Elderly: Caring for Those Who Are No Longer "Useful"

1 Corrie ten Boom, *The Hiding Place* (Grand Rapids, MI: Chosen, 2006), 63–64.

2 Pamela Rosewell, *The Five Silent Years of Corrie ten Boom* (Grand Rapids, MI: Zondervan, 1986), 156–57.

3 "In Places Where It's Legal, How Many People Are Ending Their Lives Using Euthanasia?", *The Conversation*, March 2, 2017, http://theconversation .com/in-places-where-its-legal-how-many-people-are-ending-their-lives-using -euthanasia-73755.

4 "In Places Where It's Legal."

5 Charles Lane, "How Many Botched Cases Would It Take to End Euthanasia of the Vulnerable?" Washington Post, January 24, 2018, https://www .washingtonpost.com/opinions/how-many-botched-cases-would-it-take-to -end-euthanasia-of-the-vulnerable/2018/01/24/bf311400-0124-11e8-8acf -ad2991367d9d_story.html?utm_term=.0aca834f4e04.

6 "Euthanasia and Assisted Suicide," *Encyclopedia.com*, accessed May 16, 2019, https://www.encyclopedia.com/medicine/divisions-diagnostics-and-procedures/ medicine/euthanasia.

7 Ten Boom, *Hiding Place*, 75.

8 Pamela Rosewell Moore, interview with the author, May 22, 2018.

Chapter 15: The Third Rail: Sharing the Good News with Jews

1   Corrie ten Boom, *The Hiding Place* (Grand Rapids, MI: Chosen, 2006), 88-89; also see chapter 3 in this book.
2   K. Alan Snyder, "Corrie ten Boom: A Protestant Evangelical Response to the Nazi Persecution of Jews: A Paper Presented to the Annual Conference of the Social Science History Association," Chicago, IL, November 1998, 11 21–22, https://ponderingprinciples.com/writing/Corrie_ten_Boom.pdf.
3   Ten Boom, *Hiding Place*, 29.
4   Pamela Rosewell Moore, *Life Lessons from the Hiding Place: Discovering the Heart of Corrie ten Boom* (Minneapolis: Chosen, 2004), 143–44.
5   Corrie ten Boom, *A Prisoner and Yet . . .* (repr., Fort Washington, PA: CLC Publications, 2018), 52.
6   Corrie ten Boom with Jamie Buckingham, *Tramp for the Lord* (New York: Jove Books, 1978), 101–3.
7   Corrie ten Boom, letter from Prairie View, Kansas, July 15, 1946, Collection 78 Papers of Corrie ten Boom, 1902–1997, Billy Graham Center Archives, Wheaton College.
8   "Minutes of the Board Meeting, October 22, 1974," Christians Inc., 1, Collection 78 Papers of Corrie ten Boom, 1902–1997, Billy Graham Center Archives, Wheaton College.
9   Elizabeth Sherrill, interview with the author, May 30, 2018.
10 "Purpose, Corrie ten Boom," June 5, 1976, Collection 78 Papers of Corrie ten Boom, 1902–1997, Billy Graham Center Archives, Wheaton College.
11 "Statement of Purpose," Christians Inc., July 20, 1976, Collection 78 Papers of Corrie ten Boom, 1902–1997, Billy Graham Center Archives, Wheaton College.
12 "Minutes of Meeting, Joint Meeting of Board of Directors and Executive and Administrative Committee, Christians, Incorporated," July 19, 1976, Collection 78 Papers of Corrie ten Boom, 1902–1997, Billy Graham Center Archives, Wheaton College.
13 David Neff, "Graham and the Jews: A Complex Connection," *Christianity Today*, April 2018, 68, https://www.christianitytoday.com/ct/2018/billy-graham/graham-and-jews.html.
14 Corrie ten Boom, *It's Harvest-Time!*, May–June 1968, 1, Collection 78 Papers of Corrie ten Boom, 1902–1997, Billy Graham Center Archives, Wheaton College.
15 *It's Harvest-Time!*, May-June 1968, 4–6.

Acknowledgments

1   Corrie ten Boom, *The Hiding Place* (Grand Rapids, MI: Chosen, 2006), 12.

About the Author

Stan Guthrie is the author or coauthor of six other books: *Missions in the Third Millennium: 21 Key Trends for the 21ˢᵗ Century*; *All That Jesus Asks: How His Questions Can Teach and Transform Us*; *The Sacrament of Evangelism* (coauthored with Jerry Root); *A Concise Guide to Bible Prophecy: 60 Predictions Everyone Should Know*; *God's Story in 66 Verses: Understand the Entire Bible by Focusing on Just One Verse in Each Book*; and *The Seven Signs of Jesus: God's Proof for the Open-Minded*.

Stan is an editor at large for the Colson Center for Christian Worldview, a former editor and writer for *Christianity Today*, and a former managing editor for *Evangelical Missions Quarterly* and editor of *World Pulse*. His articles, scripts, columns, and commentaries have reached millions through BreakPoint.org, ChristianHeadlines.com, *Wheaton* magazine, *Inside Journal*, *Moody*, the *Wall Street Journal*, and the Gospel Coalition. He is also a licensed minister, with a bachelor's degree in journalism (University of Florida) and a master's in intercultural studies (Columbia International University). Stan and his wife, Christine, have three children and two grandchildren and live near Chicago.

Index

About Paraclete Press

Who We Are

As the publishing arm of the Community of Jesus, Paraclete Press presents a full expression of Christian belief and practice—from Catholic to Evangelical, from Protestant to Orthodox, reflecting the ecumenical charism of the Community and its dedication to sacred music, the fine arts, and the written word. We publish books, recordings, sheet music, and video/DVDs that nourish the vibrant life of the church and its people.

What We Are Doing

Books

PARACLETE PRESS BOOKS show the richness and depth of what it means to be Christian. While Benedictine spirituality is at the heart of who we are and all that we do, our books reflect the Christian experience across many cultures, time periods, and houses of worship.

We have many series, including *Paraclete Essentials*; *Paraclete Fiction*; *Paraclete Poetry*; *Paraclete Giants*; and for children and adults, *All God's Creatures*, books about animals and faith; and *San Damiano Books*, focusing on Franciscan spirituality. Others include *Voices from the Monastery* (men and women monastics writing about living a spiritual life today), *Active Prayer*, and new for young readers: *The Pope's Cat*. We also specialize in gift books for children on the occasions of Baptism and First Communion, as well as other important times in a child's life, and books that bring creativity and liveliness to any adult spiritual life.

The MOUNT TABOR BOOKS series focuses on the arts and literature as well as liturgical worship and spirituality; it was created in conjunction with the Mount Tabor Ecumenical Centre for Art and Spirituality in Barga, Italy.

Music

The PARACLETE RECORDINGS label represents the internationally acclaimed choir *Gloriæ Dei Cantores*, the *Gloriæ Dei Cantores Schola*, and the other instrumental artists of the *Arts Empowering Life Foundation*.

Paraclete Press is the exclusive North American distributor for the Gregorian chant recordings from St. Peter's Abbey in Solesmes, France. Paraclete also carries all of the Solesmes chant publications for Mass and the Divine Office, as well as their academic research publications.

In addition, PARACLETE PRESS SHEET MUSIC publishes the work of today's finest composers of sacred choral music, annually reviewing over 1,000 works and releasing between 40 and 60 works for both choir and organ.

Video

Our video/DVDs offer spiritual help, healing, and biblical guidance for a broad range of life issues including grief and loss, marriage, forgiveness, facing death, understanding suicide, bullying, addictions, Alzheimer's, and Christian formation.

Learn more about us at our website:
www.paracletepress.com
or phone us toll-free at 1.800.451.5006

SCAN
TO
READ
MORE

You may also be interested in . . .

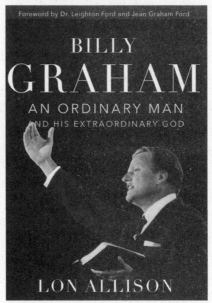

Billy Graham: An Ordinary Man and His Extraordinary God

Lon Allison
foreword by Leighton Ford and Jean Graham Ford

Hardcover | ISBN 978-1-64060-087-4 | $21.99
Trade Paperback with new Preface | ISBN 978-1-64060-205-2 | $14.99

Billy Graham said, "You have no idea how sick I get of the name Billy Graham, and how wonderful and thrilling the name Christ sounds to my ears." So why another book about him? Lon Allison, evangelist himself, and popular evangelical pastor in Wheaton, Illinois, has learned much from Billy. Allison retells the highlights of what has been, by any objective account, a fascinating life, and tells it in a way that resonates with the Graham legacy of serving God and seeking to spread the Good News.

Every stage of Graham's life is included, even the rough spots, with appreciation and a desire to answer the question: What can we learn from the life and ministry of Billy Graham? What is his legacy? What was his message and how might it still be relevant for today?

"Many will welcome the intimate details of his life revealed by Allison. Their close relationship allows the author to present a 'bird's-eye view' of the evangelist."

—David Gibson, Catholic News Service

Available at bookstores
Paraclete Press | 1-800-451-5006 | www.paracletepress.com